MY KUNG FU STROKE

A MEMOIR OF SORTS

2nd Edition

GUY LE CLAIRE

GUY LE CLAIRE

WITH HELP FROM CHRIS FRAZIER

Second Edition 2023 ISBN: 978-0-6454336-6-1

Cover Artwork: Guy Le Claire, Chris Frazier & Michael Williams

Book layout and editing:

Copyright © 2023 Guy Le Claire – mykungfu@yahoo.com

1st edition edited by Chris Frazier. 2nd edition by Guy Le Claire.

All Rights Reserved.

SPECIAL THANKS

Must be extended to wonderful people that have helped me on this journey.

Firstly the brilliant tireless work, care and commitment of Nurses, Doctors and related allied health professionals, Emergency service personnel, my Mum Carolle Anne Boyce, my Dad Guy Mackay Le ClaireMr. Chris Frazier without whose collaboration the 1st edition would not have seen the light of day, Miss Li Yin Ma, Mr. Robbin Harris, Mr. Flynn Adams, Frazier family, Sifu Yim, Sifu Pang Hon Keung William, Buddha Shakyamuni Gautama, Paramhansa Yogananda. The Gaos from Yangshuo, my SZ teacher Zhang Guang Wen, Mr. Ron Ng, Bhante Somaloka, Ike Isaacs, The Calvos, Deidre Vlahos, Venerable Kovida, Rene and Jane Buhler, Bikkhu Somaloka, Peter Scherr, Miss Lucy Lung Feng, My second wife Mrs. Bellisa Gunadhi Evans Le Claire, Dikran Balian, John Prior, Lindsay Jehan, Michael Smith, Mary Haigh, Colleen Bleathman, Samantha &Olaf Vogee,Pete Watto, my kids Nastassja Le Claire & Julien Le Claire xx

The Australian Aborigines: the original custodians of this Gondwana. The Doctors and medical staff of the HK Hospitals, The Australian Medical doctors and nurses. The Maurici family, Anna Tardent, Steve Merta, Michael Williams, Jinny Ditwald, Peter Watson, Chris Proud.

My Dad - Guy Mackay Le Claire, My Mum - Carolle Boyce Le Claire, my former wife Sylvia Chan. HKSGI. John Mallig, the HK people...GOD.Ta.

I Love and thank you all deeply from my soul...XXX. Guy Julien Le Claire

CONTENTS

SPECIAL THANKS III
CONTENTS VI
CODES IN THIS BOOK 6
FOREWORD 8
EARLY DAYS 10
    Early Family History ~ England 11
    France, Mauritius to Australia 13
    STROKES 17
    Karma or genetic or inherited 29
    DRUGS 31
    Disability 33
MY STORY 37
    Mini STROKE late May 2014 37
    STROKE 37
    HOSPITAL 39
    Me and Raymond 43
    In An Alien Spaceship 46
    RECOVERY 49
MY KUNG FU ~ ONE / PRE-STROKE 50
    BRUCE LEE 51
MY KUNG FU~TWO/POST STROKE 2015 59

Stroked & Seeking recovery in Kung Fu Activity 59

Now what is Chinese Kung Fu? 68

QI GONG aka CHI KUNG 69

What is Qi Gong? 77

Yim Sifu's huo li TAI CHI GONG 2015 78

BUDDHISM 85

Memories 91

MY KUNG FU Music One ~ Australia 120

ABOUT THE AUTHOR 181

CREDITS 182

CODES IN THIS BOOK

ABC = American born Chinese/ Australian born Chinese

adl/ado = Adelaide, capital of South Australia

Alien = thing from outer space/another world

Canto = Cantonese

Dai Lo = big brother

date = diary entry

Diu = Fuck in Cantonese

Dui = Yes in Mandarin

Face= An Asian concept of maintaining 'face', we could call it RESPECT, and acknowledgement of 'being'. A loss of face is serious, a humiliation

FB = Flashback

Ga La / Ga La Wor = subject emphasis in Cantonese expletive

g/f = girlfriend

Glec = guy le claire the author

Gig = paid music performance

ham sup lo = dirty old man/possibly really meaning wet salty person, because the Tanka women of the boats and sea, were the only ones who would fuck a foreigner in the early days of HK.

HK/hkg = Hong Kong

Hypos = Hypotheticals

JKD = Jeet Kune Do Bruce Lee's kung fu style of having no style. Founder of Mixed Martial Arts really. Combining Wing Chun drills with western boxing moves, core training and tai chi concepts.

Kung Fu = western slang for Chinese Martial Arts, a word invented and propagated by the Cantonese really means a skill honed over time.

Ly, Lyz = Li Yin.

IuniQ = Li Yins home in Shaukeiwan, HK Island

Mando = Mandarin

MMA = Mixed Martial Arts

Muso, Musoz = Musician, Musicians

Oz = Australia

Poc guy = Wanker

PR = Permanent Residence

Sifu/Shifu = Master or teacher

Seelai = 40 year old plus Chinese woman that nags and exudes negativity – a Karen?

Stroker = Stroke Survivor

Sorlo – idiot

Tai Ji = Tai Chi Chuan = Tai Ji Quan- way of the ultimate boxing, tai chi is yin yang, chuan or quan is boxing/combat.

Totes = totally

U Don noodle = You don't know

YS = Yangshuo: a village in South West China, Guangxi province

ZG = Zhong Guo – centre country= China

FOREWORD

Welcome to my 2nd revised edition of this book, first released in 2020 with the help of my brother/friend Chris Frazier during the COVID crisis lock-down, coming up to a decade of having been back in my country Australia and losing my Hong Kong citizen status, I have altered my language to keep up with modern day respects and slang to return as a good little boy(punctually) in this edition. Time granted to me by God to re-evaluate and revise this important book, especially to review and calm this work. A work is always in a state of progress. As a jazz musician we are always honing our craft, with opportunities to solidify creations "on the fly" as essentially we improvise in front of the world by performance. With this backbone a bad gig, can always be a good gig Tomorrow. Writing is restrictive in this way, historically a bad book remained a bad book? An unsuccessful book can become a good one as we now have a very different world, & in publishing too.

You may be holding this book because you are curious about kung fu or kung fu chops or k. fu strokes. This manuscript is about medical strokes – brain injury and kung fu, how I used a kung fu attitude & Chinese martial arts to get through a permanent disability from a STROKE.

This is my story, a little story & one of many, as a survivor of both 2 strokes, heart attack & COVID. I have the blessing to write & convey my experience/ story. I know we all have stories – I wish for you all to be happy, then I can fly away in the alien spaceship. Are we there yet? Are you with me... I used to think I was something special, do you? However after a time I realized I am just one of many – a demographic, I do feel as a stroke survivor I can instill some positivity in your life, even as a non qualified academic individual. Sharing some insight, understanding & awareness of stroke surviving, plain old survival is my goal. I am not a medical Doctor! I am Kung Fu Master!

Welcome to the 2nd Edition.

I am an Australian born Caucasian, half English & half Mauritian French (I look very "white" however) and an ex Hong Konger -ex due to racial barriers and the inability to maintain my hk citizen status, the inhumane scoundrels! – unable to meet my 3 year requirement to return to hong kong to keep my pr – covid etc fucked up travel ability- I unfortunately, lost my hk right, & although I left oz for 30 years, I retained my rights:).I gave HK the most productive years of my life.

I also, am an Ex professional musician, Stroker and Kung Fu enthusiast. My wish is to encourage you all to a higher plane, we all have our specific Kung Fu (a passionate skill honed over time)... each and every one of you has some special thing, you are totes awesome! Sometimes we need someone to tell us.. below is a tale of my life/ one of many…

EARLY DAYS

Duality: Mum and Dad split up when I was five. Finally going to court to claim custody of me when I was seven in 1967. In those interim years I was dragged between both of them, beginning while I was attending Neutral Bay Primary School and then Paddington Primary School, creating quite a traumatised and insecure little boy. I suffer multiple personality disorder I am Octo Polar with Traumas. The uneasiness of *dual-two* had arisen at a young age. Deafness from a measles medicine meant, a terrible hearing loss...while Dad was on his Sunday morning paper read in the park and me playing about, I established my inability to hear the birds chirping, after measles, whereas previously I would hear & point in confirmation of hearing them. This hearing debacle was confirmed by the gov Australian hearing services in York St. We could have gone at big pharma and the Dr but in those days that wasn't done. Consequently my career/employment prospects were very highly compromised, due to such hearing loss, I would not qualify for many positions, additionally I appeared a bit thick to some insensitive people, but amazingly I had a 40 year professional career in music. I could never ever understand lyrics in songs - people often thought of me as 'thick' as I couldn't understand much of what they were saying. Vocals on records weren't clear enough for me to distinguish words thus forcing me I believe, to attach to instrumental music. At the age of 13, I pursued the guitar intensively after a year or so on a tennis racket (true air guitar).

Parents split. I loved both of them equally.

The subsequent custody court case of who would "own" me, freaked me out. With friends on both sides suggesting that I tell the judge who I wanna live with... I didn't fucking know!!! In 1967 the judge awarded Dad custody of me. Mum was devastated. I freaked a bit too, but it was not like I was going to an unknown. I loved Dad immensely and Mum was totes creampied! She had me every second weekend thereafter and this became my pattern in life. Then in 1976 I lived with Mum for a year in North America.

Mum an extravagant, attractive lady, a hippy of the 60's. I always looked forward to her picking me up from the house (where I lived with Dad) in Irrawong Rd. Mona Vale. By this time I was going to Mona Vale Primary.

Relativity of simultaneity ~ Two events, simultaneous for one observer, may not be simultaneous for another observer if the observers are in relative motion.

Two of Everything ~ Diu. Two kids, Two parents, Two nationalities & abodes. Belonging to two places, always aching for the other then when you're there, wishing you were back at the first place! Fuck!! Love my Mum and Dad, I cannot choose one over the other. The duality of things began to drive me nuts.

Mum a British lady born Carolle Anne Boyce on the 24th January 1938 at 12 Clarence Rd, Teddington, Wimbledon, Kingston, London growing up during the war and London bombings, "A War Baby". Migrating to OZ at age 14, she didn't know where she was when put in a migrant camp in Ipswich QLD. After Grandpa relocated the family to Adelaide (1950's), life improved. She has a strong nature, one you wouldn't want to double-cross. She tells me I am not in line to inherit her assets. She is getting on and I worry. I help her. However, Carolle achieved an admirable career in Fashion, beginning in HK with successful fashion shows, her original georgettes gobbled up and copied (dianne freis etc.), she pushed ahead to open "Carolle Boyce Designs" in the Strand Arcade, Sydney CBD from humble beginnings in the 60s at Paddy's Market (where her creations flowed out the door to both locals and viet war rnrs).

Her fashion creations attracted clients wherever she based, & her knowledge of fabrics (among other things) is superb. Often purchasing garments and fabric from far-flung corners of the world she visited and recreating designs with the exotic fabrics cut up. Mum left Australia on a ship where I saw her off at Circular Quay on my 11th birthday. I freaked!

Early Family History ~ England

The Boyces (mums family) sailed out from Southhampton for Australia via the Suez and Sri Lanka on the SS Ormonde in 1952 (which incidentally looks ancient in pictures)settling in Qld. Grandpa moved the family to Adelaide (good move gramps). Mum blossomed there/ with gramps inviting new immigrants Russians/Polish/ Italians etc. to their crib. Mum experienced eye opening cultures & ways, I think that would down the line influence her perception of the world and work/art. Which in her 30s would amount to a lot of success & travel.

Mum's Dad, born Reginald John *"Jack"* Boyce in London in 1913. Grandpa Jack as he was known is someone I adored and remember fondly. I would visit him once a year from Sydney and enjoyed staying with him in Adelaide, Sth Australia where he had settled with his family after arriving from England via QLD. Grandpa was like a big loveable bear and was Ex-British Merchant Navy. I am half British and a crazy mix of French Mauritian/African – Indian - French Brittany. Mum's mum Grace Bizzell (I think grandma was sad & upset that her husband had dumped her & the family in Oz). She reminded me at times of the witch in the Disney cartoon *Sleeping Beauty*. Grandpa was affectionate, where as grandma wasn't so. Both grandparents have a rather complex family history, probably like a lot of migrants… names Freitag, German British interbreeding and Music talent gets bandied around but there is no clear atlas. Mum, I think has both the compassionate and aggressive traits of her parents with a good dose of Hippiedom, she truly is a 60's flower child. There is even a mountain up here in the Blue Mountains named with Grandpa… "Mt Boyce". When I was about 9, Mum met and moved in with Shanghainese born, HK & Oz bred Eddy Shen. She maintained a very successful clothes stall at Paddy's Market making shitloads of money. However with a lost custody and nagging sense to get the fuck out of Oz, those two departed Sydney on my 11th birthday for Panama (van halen!), mum believes this created a distance in our relationship, & I reckon it did. Wouldn't it for any 11 year old!!!? derr.

They never moved back home.

I reenacted this scenario with my kids in China, we went through long periods of no communication. Sadly I've heard this scenario with quite a few lonley older people. Let's Forgive! I love my kids Julien & Nastassja deeply, our kids are our and the planets future.

Julien is in cadetship with Cathay Pacific & hopes to fly those big birds that took me all around the planet in awe! Nastassja has been blessed with a mercedes benz & has a stable life. They have turned out really well!

Eddy became like my Chinese stepfather, in the old days they would pick me up for the 2nd weekend as they lived in Maroubra, we would eat in Chinatown at Canton Palace, I used to love that! Yummy. My love of Asian cuisine blossomed.

When Grandpa Jack passed on, Dad wept. Mum held a service for him where she was based at the time, in San Miguel de Allende, Mexico, where I would eventually live during 1976 with Mum & Eddy. I didn't think about Eddy's racial background, except he seemed to be occupied with money, had very creative looking hands & knew how to yummy cook. When they left Oz I felt very alone, withdrawing to the quite boring routine life with Dad in Warriewood. Mosman living was a saviour, other kids at school in a similar predicament & always something going on. Guitar became my thing, constant companion & with it I found a kungfu plus surfing & skiing. Mosman High was loaded with good guitarists. Mum is progressive.

In memoramdum of Robert Ypes, Guy Casanova, Ron Graham, Barry Stern.

France, Mauritius to Australia

The Le Claire's thought of themselves as French. The truth however was that they had been banished from Brittany, France in the early 17th Century and sent to the Island of Mauritius where they eventually became sugar cane professionals.

My Great, Great Grandfather Victor Le Claire and Great Grandfather Jean Baptiste Georges Kerdale Le Claire were both born in Port Louis, Mauritius. Jean Baptiste was a Sugar Boiler by trade and it was this occupation that enticed him initially to Australia's sugar cane belt in Queensland. Upon arrival they mostly discarded their French/Mauritian ancestry and went with the *Frenchee* vibe as that was more of an acceptable nationality status considering the White Australia policy at the time.

After moving to Mackay in Queensland, Jean Baptiste then married his Mauritian born partner Marie Noemie Collet on the 3rd January 1885. They had eight children, the second of which was my grandpa Guy Georges Le Claire who was born on the 1st July 1887.

By 1915 however, both Jean Baptiste and Marie Noemie Le Claire had resettled to the lower North Shore suburb of Chatswood in Sydney.

In Sydney Jean Baptiste became a Boot Maker until his passing on the 2nd of December 1933. The young Guy Georges Le Claire(grandpa) grew up in Mackay becoming a Tailor by trade. He married Florence Beatrice (Le Claire) and had two girls after settling in the town of Goondiwindi. This marriage dissolved around 1922, which according to a North Sydney Police Gazzette, he was charged with *Wife Desertion* and upon arrest he was duly charged and ordered to pay his wife the amount of 2 pounds support per week. He remained a Tailor till his death in Gladstone QLD on the 15th May 1955.

My father was born Guy Mackay Le Claire in Carlton, Melbourne on the 31st of May 1929 out of wedlock. His father Guy Georges had met and courted the Melbourne born Elizabeth Margaret Mackay who became his *De facto* wife. Though no official records or marriage certificate have been located, she was also known as *Le Claire* officially in subsequent Electoral Rolls records throughout Qld and NSW from 1930 onwards till her death in about 1968.

Shortly after the birth of my dad, they settled in Bundaberg QLD, later Gladstone became their home. Dad always mentioned that with the glaring Queensland sun, he himself looked like a *"Boong"* Aboriginal. He endured this racial slur his whole life and to some degree it dictated the stereotypical roles he was cast in and played throughout his acting career. (As a favoured "Baddie" Dad got to play in Homicide, Hunter, Riptide, Division Four, Poor Man's Orange, Matlock Police & A Country Practice). After I travelled the world, especially in India and Chungking Mansions, I could see by observation and witness that the original Le Claire's had indeed interbred with the Mauritian locals (African and Indian being the major populace last century). Upon settling in Sydney (late 50's), he made contact with both of his parents sides to learn more of his family history. Again it seemed to be foggy and in mystery & secrecy. Nothing is clear on both sides of my family WHO AM I? :):):)

Dad was a 1950's crooner, loved Frank Sinatra and Fred Astaire, totes encompassed by the glamour, romance and style of Hollywood circa 1940's and 50's, fine women & fashion, good manners, booze, no drugs or blatant self expression. Aussie old school.

Incredibly, during the late 1950's, my parents both arrive in Sydney as young adults, Mum from Adelaide, and Dad from Brisbane to pursue careers in the field of Drama. They are actors and were booked on the same theatre tour of the countryside beginning before Australia had television, meaning long arduous tours to country towns performing for the town folk. Mum and Dad met on one of these tours and fall in love, and here I am! I know who I Am!!!

Unfortunately seven years later in 1967 they will face each other in court in a custody battle. The judge will hand down his custody verdict. I am scared. Dad wins. I love my parents both equally.

In memoramdum of Lars Knudsen, Frances Buntz, Peter O'Shaunessy, Wynn Roberts.

I am handed over to Dad, we run away to Warriewood near Mona Vale to live. We hire a nanny part-time named Bunty (Francis Buntz) and she becomes an integral part of our lives while Dad takes up a career in his best friend Lars Knudsen's advertising company, as well as juggling acting work for Crawford Productions, Vic. Bunty brings me up on good solid Aussie foundations, respect, right attitude, manners & classic food.

Eventually we move back to the North Shore which is closer to the city and Dad's work, he'd had enough of the 190 Palm Beach/City/ Palm Beach bus trek. Happily I go back to Neutral Bay Primary, walking 4 k's a day to & from school often with my mate Chris (collaborator of this book), if we had some spare coins we would go to Jeans Fruit Palace on Wycombe Rd, Neutral Bay or Peters milk bar on Spofforth St. Cremorne to buy sweets ie: bananas, teeth, chocolate bullets, cobblers or a cold treat like a Splice or Sunnyboy. I would then carry on home to Mosman. After Primary, I went to Mosman High School, living on Avenue Rd meant there wasn't as much walking. I dug my school and Mosman. I swore to myself I wouldn't live in any other suburb. But as reality checked in - post school, and house purchasing options limited due to escalating real estate prices, alas I was not able to maintain this dream. I think that's why you can find a lot of youngish ex-North Shore people (indeed middle-class Australians) in the Blue Mountains, because it resembles the Northside somewhat but with more affordable housing. Eventually I move my family to the blue mountains (1990).

I came into this world in May of 1960, supposedly born with a heart murmur, and later in my twenties accumulating "Lipomas" and later still in my 30's as head of the guitar department at AIM, commuting daily from Katoomba to the city (2 hours one-way) upon arriving in the morning to class and suddenly my periphery of vision would narrow down to tunnel, it was quite frightening. I now think this was the beginning of a setting for a stroke later. Constant stress – work stress, career stress, sick father care/family stress, money stress, marriage stress. WHY DON'T SCHOOLS TEACH STRESS SURVIVAL!!!???

I had gone through this life crisis upon turning 30 - panic and anxiety attacks, they really were frightening, my lifestyle history had not been particularly good as I had toured with major Australian bands right through the 1980's partaking in shallow rock star antics of booze, drugs, smokes and music. For some reason I didn't deem it important to have health check-ups... Turning up to work at AIM faced with a class load of kids, I had frequent tunnel vision attacks, my vision narrowed down to peripheral, I was like wtf!? But I had to go on as we earnt our money by the hour, I now believe this was warning signs for an impending stroke – 20 years later in HK/ stressed & pressured again I succumb to 2 strokes, I had to keep going.

In 1989 Dad had had a major stroke leaving him a shell of a man he was literally "FUCKED". He suffered aphasia, blindness, paralysed limbs, mental confusion. It is sometimes opined that "how come he didn't work on improving himself?" physio etc.. Well a human with such brain loss and disability can't actually do anything, I reckon, and dad knew it. He was just waiting for God to take him (he didn't believe in God but I do), maybe that was it:). I am part of a facebook stroke survivors group and often some wished they never survived, or they really cannot deal with their predicament. I always knew I would write a book, so I had a goal, will & glad to survive.

Back to stress...There was also the mortgage (mort = *death*) stress.

Perhaps due to my parents existence in Show biz, I have always viewed life as a bit of a movie, spending time overseas kept me in the movie which tickled my fancy. As you will see in my 2nd book "My Kung FU Music" I became a bit of an actor myself, and enjoyed all the roles available.

STROKES

I've met people that shruggingly say "oh I had a stroke". They pitter patter around, but MATE you ain't had the STROKE THE ONE THAT FUCKS YOU UP BIG TIME! You may have had a pre stroke – A MINI STROKE (Transient Ischaemic Attack = TIA) also known as Pre-Stroke episode. Stroke will change your life forever, some survivors wish they never survived, I, personally am grateful for surviving as I have been supported well in both HK & Australia, & by my inner kung fu attyitude, I consider my life moving along naturally as I transition from middle age to old age the journey has been fascinating. Admittedly the constant numbness, tingling & ultra sensitivity on my left side is CRAP, like my body is divided by an invisible line from my ass crack, belly button to a definite left & right side. The "why me, why me?" mantra is non existent as I witness other older people dealing with their own limitations. Spine injured people, farmers, tradies that have given their lives to humanist work and sportspeople, now older hobble around with joints and parts that have worn out! Tai Chi would be great for youz! Strokers aren't the only ones dealing with a compromised condition, assuming and judging are terribly In Correct!

In my experience people that have had a stroke mostly have a curled hand & some spasticity, recently I found out Ram Dass had a stroke, on 1st viewing his video, his hand is curled – yup he had a stroke, inspiringly he then wrote many books as a survivor.

There are three main types of *Stroke*:

1. Ischaemic (blood clot in brain, which then destroys the affected area) – I had & my mate Oliver.

2. Transient Ischaemic Attack, Ischaemic stroke "TIA" (sometimes referred to as a 'mini-stroke') – I had

3. Hemorrhagic stroke (a bleed rupture, Aneurysm. Can also be caused from an Arteriovenous Malformation (AVM). - mate had, avm Pat Martino had. & mate Scott.

This can also include: Cerebrovascular accident (CVA) which is the sudden death of some brain cells due to lack of oxygen when the blood flow to the brain is impaired by blockage or rupture of an artery to the brain. A CVA is also referred to as a stroke. - I had

Symptoms of a stroke depend on the area of the brain affected. These can be Balance disorder, *Dysphagia* which is difficulty in swallowing and *Dysarthria* which is difficulty with speech/aphasia. One of my mates suddenly couldn't speak, his nurse friend noticed a garbled sound and quickly advised him that he is having a stroke. - Dad had all the above symptoms. In fact his condition was frightful. The severity of the Stroke and your recovery is tied in with your age. However, good attitude and having a Kung Fu will aid you immeasurably.

REMEMBER F.A.S.T.!

FACE – drooping /twisted?

ARMS – can't raise arm?

SPEECH – in ability to speak/ garbled / tongued?

TELEPHONE – telephone dial ambulance QUICKLY

FAST... the stroke mantra!!!

"If you don't know at 26 why you've had a stroke it can be pretty disabling to think- " is it going to happen again?"

"I probably under appreciate my story a fair bit. I've never fully realized the complexity of what I've achieved "maybe I am a bit of a miracle" (quotes from online)

What is a stroke? A Mayo Clinic expert explains

Learn more from neurologist Robert Brown, M.D.

Show transcript for video What is a stroke? A Mayo Clinic expert explains

An ischemic stroke occurs when the blood supply to part of the brain is interrupted or reduced, preventing brain tissue from getting oxygen and nutrients. Brain cells begin to die in minutes.

A stroke is a medical emergency, and prompt treatment is crucial. Early action can reduce brain damage and other complications.

The good news is that many fewer Americans die of stroke now than in the past. Effective treatments can also help prevent disability from stroke.

Symptoms

If you or someone you're with may be having a stroke, pay particular attention to the time the symptoms began. Some treatment options are most effective when given soon after a stroke begins.

Signs and symptoms of stroke include:

- **Trouble speaking and understanding what others are saying.** You may experience confusion, slur words or have difficulty understanding speech.

- **Paralysis or numbness of the face, arm or leg.** You may develop sudden numbness, weakness or paralysis in the face, arm or leg. This often affects just one side of the body. Try to raise both your arms over your head at the same time. If one arm begins to fall, you may be having a stroke. Also, one side of your mouth may droop when you try to smile.

- **Problems seeing in one or both eyes.** You may suddenly have blurred or blackened vision in one or both eyes, or you may see double.

- **Headache.** A sudden, severe headache, which may be accompanied by vomiting, dizziness or altered consciousness, may indicate that you're having a stroke.

- **Trouble walking.** You may stumble or lose your balance. You may also have sudden dizziness or a loss of coordination.

When to see a doctor

Seek immediate medical attention if you notice any signs or symptoms of a stroke, even if they seem to come and go or they disappear completely. Think "FAST" and do the following:

- **Face.** Ask the person to smile. Does one side of the face droop?

- **Arms.** Ask the person to raise both arms. Does one arm drift downward? Or is one arm unable to rise?

- **Speech.** Ask the person to repeat a simple phrase. Is his or her speech slurred or strange?

- **Time.** If you observe any of these signs, call 911 or emergency medical help immediately.

Causes

There are two main causes of stroke: a blocked artery (ischemic stroke) or leaking or bursting of a blood vessel (hemorrhagic stroke). Some people may have only a temporary disruption of blood flow to the brain, known as a transient ischemic attack (TIA), that doesn't cause lasting symptoms.

Ischemic stroke

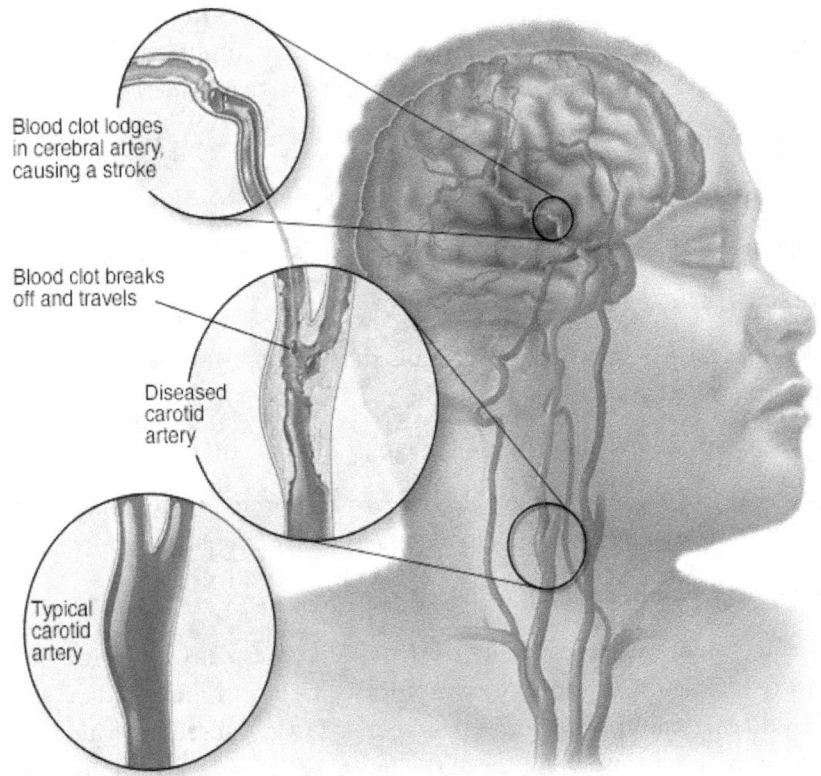

This is the most common type of stroke. It happens when the brain's blood vessels become narrowed or blocked, causing severely reduced blood flow (ischemia). Blocked or narrowed blood vessels are caused by fatty deposits that build up in blood vessels or by blood clots or other debris that travel through the bloodstream, most often from the heart, and lodge in the blood vessels in the brain.

Some initial research shows that COVID-19 infection may increase the risk of ischemic stroke, but more study is needed.

Hemorrhagic stroke

Hemorrhagic stroke occurs when a blood vessel in the brain leaks or ruptures. Brain hemorrhages can result from many conditions that affect the blood vessels. Factors related to hemorrhagic stroke include:

- Uncontrolled high blood pressure

- Overtreatment with blood thinners (anticoagulants)

- Bulges at weak spots in your blood vessel walls (aneurysms)

- Trauma (such as a car accident)

- Protein deposits in blood vessel walls that lead to weakness in the vessel wall (cerebral amyloid angiopathy)

- Ischemic stroke leading to hemorrhage

A less common cause of bleeding in the brain is the rupture of an irregular tangle of thin-walled blood vessels (arteriovenous malformation).

Transient ischemic attack (TIA)

A transient ischemic attack (TIA) — sometimes known as a ministroke — is a temporary period of symptoms similar to those in a stroke. A TIA doesn't cause permanent damage. A TIA is caused by a temporary decrease in blood supply to part of the brain, which may last as little as five minutes.

Like an ischemic stroke, a TIA occurs when a clot or debris reduces or blocks blood flow to part of the nervous system.

Seek emergency care even if you think you've had a TIA because your symptoms got better. It's not possible to tell if you're having a stroke or TIA based only on the symptoms. If you've had a TIA, it means you may have a partially blocked or narrowed artery leading to the brain. Having a TIA increases your risk of having a full-blown stroke later.

Risk factors

Many factors can increase the risk of stroke. Potentially treatable stroke risk factors include:

Lifestyle risk factors

- Being overweight or obese

- Physical inactivity

- Heavy or binge drinking

- Use of illegal drugs such as cocaine and methamphetamine

Medical risk factors

- High blood pressure

- Cigarette smoking or secondhand smoke exposure

- High cholesterol

- Diabetes

- Obstructive sleep apnea

- Cardiovascular disease, including heart failure, heart defects, heart infection or irregular heart rhythm, such as atrial fibrillation

- Personal or family history of stroke, heart attack or transient ischemic attack

- COVID-19 infection

Other factors associated with a higher risk of stroke include:

- **Age** — People age 55 or older have a higher risk of stroke than do younger people.

- **Race or ethnicity** — African Americans and Hispanics have a higher risk of stroke than do people of other races or ethnicities.

- **Sex** — Men have a higher risk of stroke than do women. Women are usually older when they have strokes, and they're more likely to die of strokes than are men.

- **Hormones** — Use of birth control pills or hormone therapies that include estrogen increases risk.

- Stress I believe stress contributes to medical episodes.

Complications

A stroke can sometimes cause temporary or permanent disabilities, depending on how long the brain lacks blood flow and which part is affected. Complications may include:

Paralysis or loss of muscle movement. You may become paralyzed on one side of the body, or lose control of certain muscles, such as those on one side of the face or one arm.

Difficulty talking or swallowing. A stroke might affect control of the muscles in the mouth and throat, making it difficult for you to talk clearly, swallow or eat. You also may have difficulty with language, including speaking or understanding speech, reading, or writing.

Memory loss or thinking difficulties. Many people who have had strokes experience some memory loss. Others may have difficulty thinking, reasoning, making judgments and understanding concepts.

Emotional problems. People who have had strokes may have more difficulty controlling their emotions, or they may develop depression.

Pain. Pain, numbness or other unusual sensations may occur in the parts of the body affected by stroke. For example, if a stroke causes you to lose feeling in the left arm, you may develop an uncomfortable tingling sensation in that arm.

Changes in behavior and self-care ability. People who have had strokes may become more withdrawn. They may need help with grooming and daily chores.

Prevention

Knowing your stroke risk factors, following your health care provider's recommendations and adopting a healthy lifestyle are the best steps you can take to prevent a stroke. If you've had a stroke or a transient ischemic attack (TIA), these measures might help prevent another stroke. The follow-up care you receive in the hospital and afterward also may play a role.

Many stroke prevention strategies are the same as strategies to prevent heart disease. In general, healthy lifestyle recommendations include:

Controlling high blood pressure (hypertension). This is one of the most important things you can do to reduce your stroke risk. If you've had a stroke, lowering your blood pressure can help prevent a subsequent TIA or stroke. Healthy lifestyle changes and medications are often used to treat high blood pressure.

Lowering the amount of cholesterol and saturated fat in your diet. Eating less cholesterol and fat, especially saturated fat and trans fats, may reduce buildup in the arteries. If you can't control your cholesterol through dietary changes alone, your doctor may prescribe a cholesterol-lowering medication.

Quitting tobacco use. Smoking raises the risk of stroke for smokers and nonsmokers exposed to secondhand smoke. Quitting tobacco use reduces the risk of stroke.

Managing diabetes. Diet, exercise and losing weight can help you keep your blood sugar in a healthy range. If lifestyle factors don't seem to be enough to control your diabetes, your doctor may prescribe diabetes medication.

Maintaining a healthy weight. Being overweight contributes to other stroke risk factors, such as high blood pressure, cardiovascular disease and diabetes.

Eating a diet rich in fruits and vegetables. A diet containing five or more daily servings of fruits or vegetables may reduce the risk of stroke. The Mediterranean diet, which emphasizes olive oil, fruit, nuts, vegetables and whole grains, may be helpful.

Exercising regularly. Aerobic exercise reduces the risk of stroke in many ways. Exercise can lower blood pressure, increase the levels of good cholesterol, and improve the overall health of the blood vessels and heart. It also helps you lose weight, control diabetes and reduce stress. Gradually work up to at least 30 minutes of moderate physical activity — such as walking, jogging, swimming or bicycling — on most, if not all, days of the week.

Drinking alcohol in moderation, if at all. Heavy alcohol consumption increases the risk of high blood pressure, ischemic strokes and hemorrhagic strokes. Alcohol may also interact with other drugs you're taking. However, drinking small to moderate amounts of alcohol, such as one drink a day, may help prevent ischemic stroke and decrease the blood's clotting tendency. Talk to your doctor about what's appropriate for you.

Treating obstructive sleep apnea (OSA). Your doctor may recommend a sleep study if you have symptoms of OSA — a sleep disorder that causes you to stop breathing for short periods repeatedly during sleep. Treatment for OSA includes a device that delivers positive airway pressure through a mask to keep the airway open while you sleep.

Avoiding illegal drugs. Certain street drugs, such as cocaine and methamphetamine, are established risk factors for a TIA or a stroke.

Preventive medications

If you've had an ischemic stroke or a TIA, your doctor may recommend medications to help reduce your risk of having another stroke. These include:

Anti-platelet drugs. Platelets are cells in the blood that form clots. Anti-platelet drugs make these cells less sticky and less likely to clot. The most commonly used anti-platelet medication is aspirin. Your doctor can help you determine the right dose of aspirin for you.

After a TIA or minor stroke, your doctor may give you aspirin and an anti-platelet drug such as clopidogrel (Plavix) for a period of time to reduce the risk of another stroke. If you can't take aspirin, your doctor may prescribe clopidogrel alone.

Anticoagulants. These drugs reduce blood clotting. Heparin is fast acting and may be used short-term in the hospital.

Slower-acting warfarin (Jantoven) may be used over a longer term. Warfarin is a powerful blood-thinning drug, so you'll need to take it exactly as directed and watch for side effects. You'll also need to have regular blood tests to monitor warfarin's effects.

Several newer blood-thinning medications (anticoagulants) are available for preventing strokes in people who have a high risk. These medications include dabigatran (Pradaxa), rivaroxaban (Xarelto), apixaban

(Eliquis) and edoxaban (Savaysa). They're shorter acting than warfarin and usually don't require regular blood tests or monitoring by your doctor. These drugs are also associated with a lower risk of bleeding complications compared to warf

The actual event of having the stroke was quite painless – especially compared to when I had a heart attack – stroke just knocks you out,like becoming lifeless unless you wake up – I did – then your fucked, heart attack I was all conscious and noticed my body changing totes out of my control freaky. I reckon stroke death would be nice. Also the flu influenza was freaky, I was asymptomatic in Covid. Our paramedics & health officers are totes awesome! They deserve their wage increase! I love them!!!

Are we there yet?

Clearly the survivors who work at recovery, are the ones to recover, one cannot sit around moping, you have to work hard at it, and adjust your attitude/thinking. The hardest part of stroke I find is dealing day to day with the permanency of it. I honestly believed one day I would wake up and be back in a normal body. Pursuing the ole kung fu determinedly was my action to attain this freedom, however de medical is correct dis is de permanent. The nerve pain included in this stroke condition is overwhelming sometimes, constant tingling/numbing sensation on affected side. Physical intimacy is precluded. Is Sciatica or early sciatica a stroke warner? Stress is the one!

When Dad suffered a very severe stroke in 1989 the poor bastard, he was only 59 years old. I was busy in the Aussie pop band *Eurogliders*. Initially the police stated 'assault' due to the condition of his flat with broken windows and overturned furniture, blood everywhere. This made me furious, with an inner unknown ability to hunt and kill a perpetrator. With all that anger and uncertainty, the Police told me to get over to the Royal North Shore Hospital. I jumped in my red Ford Cortina in Marrickville (where I was living) and by the time I was on the Sydney Harbour Bridge in orderly traffic, I was freaking out. It was all too much, the medical team told me Dad was not in a good way with permanent damage, he would not be a good look upon being released from hospital & he wasn't. I was determined to save him as best I could and did.

Now, after what I have personally experienced, I believe he first suffered a T.I.A *mini Stroke,* losing his facilities and in the ensuing three days alone in his flat, frustratingly struggled with his condition, unable to stand or walk, he knocked over all the furniture leaving his flat in a total mess, it then manifested into a major Stroke. It is essential to get a stroke victim in with the medical/ambulance etc! fast!

Interestingly the last entry in his Diary, dated the 2nd of January, 1989 *"more heart palpitations in the early hours."* Coincidentally, he had been seeing a Chinese/Australian doctor but felt that particular doctor wasn't able to correctly diagnose his issue. Dad had a bit of a mistrust with Doctors. With that last entry, I strongly suspect he was also suffering AF (*Atrial Fibrillation*) brought about by the added stress from a recent career change. Af is a leading stroke contributor, recently the founder of Dumble amps – Howard – passed away from af leading to stroke.

Atrial Fibrillation:

The heart's upper chambers (atria) beat out of coordination with the lower chambers (ventricles).

This condition may have no symptoms, but when symptoms do appear they include palpitations, shortness of breath and fatigue.

Treatments include drugs, electrical shock (cardioversion procedure) and minimally invasive surgery (ablation).

It is estimated that 12.1 million people in the United States will have AFib in 2030. In 2019, AFib was mentioned on 183,321 death certificates and was the underlying cause of death in 26,535 of those deaths. People of European descent are more likely to have AFib than African Americans.

If you or anyone you know has AF, it could be paroxysmal af or permanent af. Both can be dangerous if left untreated. Every 40 seconds someone in the US has a stroke & every 3.5 seconds someone dies of stroke, Blacks have the highest death rate due to stroke. My af peaked at 160bpm and a chest that heaved, it was freaky, I then had to self inject needles into my gut twice a day which was really not my cup of tea, & take warfarin.

Stroke is a leading cause of serious long term disability.

There is much to discover & research on the web, I suggest you do.

Two things –

1. do not avoid your Doctor & or medical people if you are sick or suffering/ by all means seek a second opinion if it makes you feel better

2. Stress is a very bad condition for health.

Dad's post stroke condition totes freaked me out, no doubt it freaked him out too/ he lost the mojo and was totes helpless, such a horrible state to be in. Whenever he saw me there was joy. He was affected to the point of not being able to speak, communicate, see or read. A shell of his former self in fact it was like he had already died. Eventually, he was able to nod a simple *yes* or *no*. Dad, having never fully recovered, eventually passed away in May 2001.

I believe I overcame the restrictions of stroke with hemi paralysis, through my kung fu attitude, mental ability to keep positively engaged, activity & drinking wine in moderation:).

With my determination to follow Chinese kung fu / to physically overcome my paralysis and regain movement, balance & independence! That's the reason why this book is called "MY KUNG FU STROKE" Stroker on a kung fu path! You can too!!! the beauty of life is we can do anything. Meditate, play yoga, go down the beach, sit in an airplane, pollute, not pollute, save conservation. Get off ya arses lazy fucks:)

Karma or genetic or inherited

My Dad's stroke terribly disabled him possibly due to karma some may say. People have the need to say *"oh karmic"* but is it karma? as the west has identified – like you/he/she got this or deserved this cause u were an asshole or something similar/ ' they will get their Karma'. Or is it in fact in ones genes or simply an inherited tradition or action? Buddhism considers 'cause & effect.'

Dad thought all activities outside the European wing were Baloney or suspect, by following the French and Aussie ways he drank, ate meat, cheeses, etc. building potential high cholesterol and clogged arteries. Any

Hare Krishna food or Vegan alternative was out. I have to agree with Nichiren that a lot of what may be happening to you is not genetic as passed down through ones' genes or medical family history, BUT by following ones family tradition and habits... your old man drank and ate copious amounts of red meat you probably do, and if he got sick with "?", you probably will, or your Mum cooked rice and fish, so will you.

All those years ago both my parents loved their grog. Dad had casks of wine and they both celebrated with booze as he loved to get all Frenchee due to his insecurity as a fuzzy haired dark olive skinned guy. Cognac and apple shit, French lessons with Alliance Francaise de Sydney and piss-ups out the back with Jean Marc.

Pernod, Calvados, *Mumm* Champagne, Pâté fromage etc, mais qui!? Non? Qui. Mum would have boxes of wine delivered to her mini Billy Fields mansion behind Bondi Junction for piss-ups, aptly named "dinner parties". Dad and Lars were childhood mates since Gladstone, coming from an Aussie culture of beers down the pub after a days work, piss up and carry on! Grown-up and in the advertising world with dollars rolling in this way and that. Total piss-up nights, until one night Rolf and I decided to leave 'em to run down to Kings Cross to busk with bottles of Brandivino or Blackberry nip. It wasn't in our genes but in our jeans, we had money to buy the shit. Growing up in an affluent suburb like Mosman where the parents were happy to shell out the *dosh* to get rid of the kids for a time while they pissed up. *"Here's 50 bucks, go down to the Big 20 Burger joint"*. That and bags of Grass. So in comes the darn drugs. That wasn't in their genes. One of the hippest parts of Mosman High School was smoking weed and spotting hash. Other kids were dabbling in acid and smack. Needles scared the fuck out of me.

FB

...Linus and me are doing lots of coke, he is trying to educate me in his way, by exposing me to lots of music - African, South American, American urban culture stuff, I'm taking it in but we both notice the little packet is running low, so he makes a call and more is delivered. You can get anything you want in the ole honkers. Linus is attached to the concept of "harmolodics", espoused by Ornette Coleman, indeed he has a strong

Jamaladeen Tacuma element in his playing, Linus has a strong organic Ali Farka Toure – ness to his playing also. He likes to wear Issey Miyake clothes and is often mistaken as a crossdresser in this primarily conservative city. However we do many great gigs together. He is only one of many characters in this incredible city of HK...

DRUGS

I started to think I'm really hooked on this shit, how can I get off the shit? I can say I indulged for quite a while, it was the nature of life in HK... (and also touring in major bands in Oz during the 80's). HK networking/fast paced -HK Drink, drink, network, network, hang crap on get gigs gigs, run out of energy, score for a pep, in the dunny snort, come out ready to finalise that future gigs contract. This routine 7 nights a week with performing on most nights became the routine. I was in a pickle. But somehow by the grace of God I just stopped. Just like that. Where am I going with this book? Are we there yet?:) I don't know, but I trudge along, wanna read some more?

Lying in bed with a heart pumping like a mutha fucka, little did I know that I was setting up future heart disease. This dumb *"ROCK lifestyle"* starting in Sydney lasted a good 5 years. And by some chance I just stopped, there was no "my kung fu" or religious experience or lack of money. Just stopped like that. Except for one time before a gig I rated highly and with nerves, *a friend?* offered me a line in the dunny, after which during an intense guitar solo, I think my heart went into Atrial Fibrillation big time. Not long after that in 2012, I was flying to Adelaide to visit family and start a tour with the clean *Matt Finish*. Also my then Girlfriend, an Indonesian domestic helper holed up in HK - domestic helpers, the pretty ones use their pussies to make a buck or find a wealthy hubby or sponsor... left me, I couldn't fucken believe it *"she left **ME**, Guy Le Claire!"*, but it was for real! I threw her out and got myself into a habit of a bottle or two of NZ Sauvignon Blanc a day while listening to Jason Mraz and reading Red Hot Chilli Peppers singer Anthony Keidis' book *Scar Tissue* (bad move). Listening to Mraz's *Only Human and Beautiful Mess*, totes fucked me up, I was in the darkest sadness, but I wallowed in it, I kinda liked it. Sorlo.

The Adelaide local doctor said "You've got a serious problem" and I could see it as my heart pounded in my chest, it was quite terrifying to look at. Finally in Sydney, bandleader/friend John Prior sent me over to his local GP where she promptly sent me off up to Newtown to have a Cardiogram.

Once that was done the nurse couldn't make head or tails of it, so she faxed and called the head office. They said get that man straight to hospital in a car. So John ran me up to the Royal Prince Alfred Hospital, we went into emergency and once they looked at the ECG I was immediately admitted into emergency room. With so many different Doctors and nurses and no family, I checked myself out later that night and went back to Johns. Next day saw GP and she referred me to heart specialist Dr. Jo-Dee Lattimore. I got on well with her and luckily she bulk billed me, as well as set a path to see if the heart might settle down. I was on Warfarin (a blood thinner to help reduce risk of clots/stroke) and every day had to get my blood checked. Well it seemed my blood wasn't thin enough, so I then had to inject myself with super long syringe/needles twice a day. I was freaking plus I had a tour to make...

I wanted to go home as my house in Sai Kung as it was like my refuge and HK was now my home.

After a cardio version procedure my af settled down & I managed to do the *Matt Finish* tour 2012 though many of our gigs were cancelled because pre-ticket sales were low or non-existent and probably the publican didn't wanna risk it and pulled the plug. I remember a couple of good gigs at "The Blue Room" and "Lizottes". Touring and playing with John Prior, David Adams and Harry Brus was always a great pleasure. Dr. Lattimore began talking about *Catheter Ablation* (which really freaked me out) and a procedure date was set for a cardioversion, which was done successfully at the time.

Singapore Airlines agreed to help me out with my flight back to HK. This doctor prior to cardioversion told me my heart is acting like I'm running a marathon as it beat at 160 bpm just by standing still and that I need plenty of rest. It was quite frightening.

My daughter had been accepted into Sydney Uni, so she accompanied me into the hospital on the day of procedure, of course I was nervous, and really wanted to get it over and done with. We two waited for ages, as the anaesthetist was very busy, they rolled me off into a room where I would be put to sleep. I could see the two Cardioversion prongs like 2 irons, then the anaesthetist arrived. He began doing his thing and he reminded me of my good mate drummer Nicholas McBride, I said "hey I'm not gay, but can I hold your hand?" he said "ok" and I was out! Waking up in the ward where Stassy had been waiting, I felt gravity and heavy with the young trainee Doctor coming out saying "it was successful!".

I arrived back in HK actively seeking employment and getting it. With no girlfriend, I was longing... Then my fellow music comrade Peter Scherr from *Creative Music China* suggested I meet a mainland girl - LiYin, who was now living in HK. I had had quite a number of mainland girlfriends and having left the mainland after 3 years there with a destroyed relationship and a nagging feel of having been ripped off (I still couldn't really effectively defend myself – after 3 years totes focussed on Tai Chi). I was not in the most "up" mood about meeting LiYin. We met and had a lovely afternoon at Clearwater Bay Beach and a past-life experience at Popcorn Plaza T.K.O.

Two months later she moved into my village house. All kung fu was out although with Frenchman Oliver Smith (a survivor) we created *HK Musicians Health* and guided about 5 people/musoz through some Qi Gong/Tai Chi and Ving Tsun. I was also teaching tai chi to some students and teachers for ESF School but I wasn't training hard. I seemed to have enough money for the rent/food/outgoings and booze, I was back on my Suave Blanc scheming the release of my new music... I decided to release 3 CDs with financial help from LiYin. It was done. Each CD was representative of my work up to this point. **"GleC- ROCK HITZ"** - *History*, **"GleC Trio 2"** with Scott Dodd and Robbin Harris *(jazz)*, **"GleC- SOLO 3"** - *acoustic (world music)*.

Disability

Unfortunately the experience of having a Stroke, may leave us with a permanent disability. We will need to find avenues of income & support. Disableds need support & advocacy, Australia has support mechanisms in place with a disability pension, that amounts to a fair sum, as well as N.D.I.S.

– National Disability Insurance Scheme (available to under 60 year olds- otherwise you need age care), which may allocate an annual sum into a trust account to enable you to hire support workers/ home care/ activity/engage in therapies etc. With planning and positive outcomes, Australia is a very good place to be as a disabledderer, I believe involving oneself in this burgeoning employment circle will pay high dividends. If I was starting out in employment I would def go down this employment pathway. It's a win win because the participant and worker gain value & quality of life. Incredibly at age 63 I register as a support worker ! Strokers are generally dealing with a dead part of their brain(we need to retrain ourselves & be mindful of brain plasticity) creating blockage to send nerve signals to moving body parts & brain fog, many of us cannot handle over stimulation, strokers are not the only ones going through all this disability drama. Disability covers a broad spectrum of individuals from brain injuries, spinal/ back injuries/ accidents involving Workers, Sports, amputations, LIFE so us strokers are not the only ones dig?

The hard truth for disableds is living with this permanent disability, previously once in a life before we were active physically, work-wise etc. One is now 'unable', with frustrating limitations and independence. Another annoying issue is like 'gayhate' crimes as there are certain individuals that have the need for 'disabled hate crime' – bullying, annoying, abusing, teasing and being downright arseholes! And they get away with it! Get the police powers! There exists a jealousy, also. I am continually having tussles with my mother with issues of money and respect. She can be a bitch!

Another unpleasant factor of disability -is people, friends & families perception of the disabled individual, a stigma bu hao la- not good!, there needs to be some adjustment in outsiders & family perceptions and expectations, drop ya assuming judgemental shit! Chaps like Dylan Alcott are admirable I love him. Be respectful & courteous. Drop de disabled stigma.

As a disabled dude, simple things like walking on the sand or tall grass, walking barefoot (hurts), hanging the washing using both arms/legs freely, household chores become problematic if not impossible, we are often subjected to immense frustration & difficulty in maintaining ' normal' relationships. Strokers are recovering mainly due to brain plasticity - and dedicated hardworking exercise, commitment & determination. Re 'plasticity' check out authors N. Doidge and Peter Levine 'Stronger after stroke' books. U ought to investigate yourself, as in addition to our sicknesses & being monitored by the medical, we need to be actively involved also. Helping ourselves, not only leaving it to everyone/ thing around us. You don't become KungFu Master by relying on others, one has to put in the hard yakka! I recommend engaging with community/ sharing is a wonderful & important act. Even if we fail we had a good experience. At this moment I would like to thank my NDIS Team, u know who u r. taaaa x

One final immense frustration for all, especially older people & disablederers is the lack of personal service! Everything is online!!!FUCKen diu lei lo moz! Bring back real people & service ga laaaaaa

February 2012   Oz~HK pre stroke

My Atrial Fibrillation began to get out of control when I arrived in Adelaide from HK to visit Mum and begin a tour of Oz with *Matt Finish* in 2012. Flying down from HK, I noticed my heart heaving in my chest. I had AF full-time!160bpm at rest. Terrifying. I made that tour and It was only after a cardioversion procedure at RPAH that I was then allowed to fly back to Hong Kong.

Back in HK, I was working hard to keep the bills at bay having just completed the *Matt Finish* tour. Over the next 2 years I began composing and recording music then organising for three new *GleC (GleC=guy le claire)*CDs to be released. As these were my first releases in a few years, I was Totes stressed about it and probably drinking too much. I went back into Atrial Fibrillation. AF is a killer.

adoption/orphans

2014 fall - Hong Kong

HK is a hard living place with all kinds of pollutants (and mutants). One particular evening with the prospect of an under-rehearsed gig that night, I didn't feel too well so I decided to have a lie down. Ducking fell asleep and awoke at 11pm. Gig was over. I missed the ducking gig! So the local little tyrant who I was supposed to play with decided, *"Fuck you, I douse you with petrol"* and totally cyber bullied me on social media with all the other locals joining in to absolutely ruin my professional music reputation. Welcome to Hong Kong. More fucking Stress! At this moment, I would like to thank this individual for the path set for me, in some ways surviving a stroke is liberating. Ram Dass and Hugh Hefner have mentioned their strokes were like a 'stroke of luck' I often feel the same. Hk mate, I wish you all the best! No worries. Shit happens.

MY STORY...

Mini STROKE late May 2014

Falling to the floor surprisingly out of nowhere one afternoon at my house in *Mang Kung Uk, Clearwater Bay, HK*, I didn't feel it coming but I did have Atrial Fibrillation, on the floor my whole left side was paralysed. I thought *"what the fuck!"*, but somehow I managed to slide along the floor by grabbing the legs of the table with my good arm and grab my mobile and call my amazing girlfriend Li Yin, she rushed over in a cab. By the time she got there, I asked her to pick me up and plop me on a chair, after which, my left side started to move again. Stubbornly/stupidly I refused to go to hospital(typical Alpha Aussie Male) Biggest Mistake!. I had suffered a *TIA*, "Transient Ischaemic Attack" also noted as a *mini stroke* and precursor to STROKE (I had never heard of TIA). The next day, my Sai Kung doctor Clifford Loo (UNSW) said *"TIA"* but with the locals bad English pronunciation, I thought he said, "CIA"... Well that's what it sounded like, What the fuck...!?

Well this particular doctor didn't insist at the time to send me to the hospital for an MRI so unfortunately I was none the wiser. If you think you may have FAST symptoms. You go to get MRI!!! is what you do ok? - glec.

STROKE

Anyway, one week later while over at Li Yin's place in *Shaukeiwan* on the Sunday evening of June 1st 2014, I dropped again in her kitchen, this time I *was* fucked. It felt like a total shut down on my left side, there was no pain (unlike the heart attack I would have later in 2023), just extreme helplessness. I had had an Ischaemic Stroke CVA...*the aliens had abducted me...* to do some tests and returned me as a stroker. Did you know in the US, someone has a stroke every 45 seconds. It's on the rise in Asia, especially *mini strokes* - a pandemic. Luckily with emergency treatment, mini strokes

37

appear to be more treatable with good recovery prospects. Australia's stroke statistics are How many Australians have had a stroke? **In 2018, an estimated 387,000 Australians aged 15 and over (1.3% of the population) had experienced a stroke at some time in their lives**, based on self-reported data from the ABS Survey of Disability, Ageing and Carers (ABS 2019).29 Sept 2021 These may be ministroke inclusive I don't know.

Stroke rates improve with prompt medical treatment. The frightful truth is that with young humans glued to phones, computers and games and no physical exercise, crap diet, obesity on the rise, we are headed for a horrific endemic. I have met many early older people (50-60) that have told me they had a stroke, it turns out they were more min-stroke episodes, which means the percentage of recovery is good for mini-strokes as they are less serious often having no permanent damage like permanent damage strokes, which are the most frustrating, Mini strokers - don't assume because a stroker you met is like you DIG!? – as a member of the stroke recovery facebook group, a lot of members who have paralysis can get very negative wanting to give up, or wishing they died instead of survived.[1]

When the ambulance arrived I felt so comforted by their strong hands, taking me in, just like Manu Bennett, *Allanon* the druid in *The Shannara Chronicles series*. Once in the emergency ward I kept screaming "Li Yin! Li Yin!!" I was terrified & MRI'd... awoke the next day in the stroke ward. I would remain here in Pamela Youde Nethersole Eastern Hospital HK for the next near 2 months.

One of our human faults is assuming things, and I assumed that since I was alive I would get better and back to playing guitar and working - I have been a professional creative musician for 40 years and quite a proud one, particularly here in HK. I had supported myself financially without govt assistance. I believe I had impacted the HK music scene in a positive way, I created employment, creative projects and opportunities for other musicians, but it was all over with this stroke. It is coming up to 10 years later now (I've read 10 years after is a good innings – c ya!:) and I cannot play at my past level, I can play but it's fucked. I've let it go.

HOSPITAL

Stroke Ward: Pamela Youde Eastern Nethersole Hospital HK

Anyway, here at the hospital, we all got wheeled out twice a day for physio and occupational therapies. Mr. Tam (oz trained) the physio who I liked a lot, taught me to walk again (I couldn't walk) and just stand up (placing your feet strategically in the correct place). It was terrifying as I had always suffered vertigo, and when I stood up I felt that I was going to fall, like in those falling dreams when you fall, for all (Dreamworld OILS), also Jackson (the assistant) was bloody good especially when I was an out-patient rehaber, didn't see Mr. Tam in out-patient, but visited him once when I could walk independently.

In the beginning I was always joking around. Everything was funny. Within my first week in hospital, the head nurse told us my Haematoma (trauma from injury) had gone. I have had serious "nothin funny" phases in my life so I am not all jokes and candy, like when I used to practice guitar 8 hours a day, learning Wing Chun – Kung Fu, listening and respecting the elders dialogue, but with this stroke business it was all a *Hooo Haaaa*. I was Mr Joker. Perhaps my brain and conscious couldn't accept it so I went all *spazzo*.

I shared the stroke ward with *Li Ka Shing*: a boy who suffered brain damage from a car crash. An old bloke from Shek O that had fallen off a ladder and bumped his head and looked like *Sun Wu Kong* from the *Monkey King*, and then there was General Guang Tou - the noisiest bugger ever! To me he looked like a *Guo/Kuo Min Tang General*. I started inventing weird suspicious characters out of the resident patients. There were spies and law people, everything I looked at like clouds and curtains had faces or figures, it would keep me constantly occupied and still does. Li Yin was super worried.

The nurse and staff were nice and competent here, no politics yet, that came later at rehab hospital. In the stroke ward we were lifted by hoist on rails attached to the ceiling a few times a week to shower/wash. No one could move anything, we were also in nappies. That was just horrible. Slowly my neighbours were being taken away, later I found out to the rehab hospital. And after nearly 2 months, my turn came.

Rehab Hospital: Tung Wah Eastern Hospital HK

On Saturday 19th July, while strapped to a bed, I was wheeled outside and got my first taste of the outside world in 7 weeks. Going down the Eastern Freeway side of HK, past Li Yin's place and her office, was an odd feeling. HK harbour on the right, with the Nine Dragons Mountain in the distance separating Kowloon from the New Territories. Cement blocks on the left, a place I called home for 20 years. (Recently I picked up a book by an Aussie who grew up in Kowloon with the Michael Hutchence INXS family, I was shocked that he thought Kowloon consisted of 8 hills, *Kow* is Gau = 9... Derr! *loon* is *loong* = dragon – Kowloon- 9 dragon). The language abilities on both sides - with Chinese HKers and hk ex-pats is terribly appalling!

Upon my arrival at Tung Wah Eastern Hospital at the back of one of the most populated areas in *dee vorld*, Causeway Bay (Tung Lo Wan Rd), I am greeted by a very attractive nurse, who keeps giggling and saying *"You handsome"*, then wheeled into the rehab ward during visiting hours. Everyone including more attractive nurses turn around to check me out, the *"Gwai Lo"* has arrived.

I become self conscious. My whole tenure in hkg *hospitaldom* is local and Govt sponsored, I have no insurance so I am not in a private scheme. Luckily I have PR (permanent resident) status, meaning some local government support. Settling beside General Guang Tou who is now chained to his bed, I spend the next few weeks kept awake by the Generals manic behaviour. Finally after some complaining and Mums suggestion to *"just give 'im a shot and knock 'im out"*, I am moved across the ward near the entrance opposite Raymond and Sifu, a much better position. Sun Wu Kong now has things on his hands similar to that which dogs wear like a muzzle because he is trying to continually pull out the tubes, I felt bad for him in his frustration. Li Yin visits me everyday bringing healthy home cooked food and her uplifting spirit. I have read "Standing Up" by Australian Kathleen Jordan and she talks about how important it was for her to have her family *"there"*. I'm divorced, and...

FB: 2003 Australia/HK. Pre stroke..

I have just been in Melbourne Australia, enrolling my son and daughter into schools, finalising the property my wife and I have bought in Footscray. I then go to Adelaide where my Mum lives, in ado I board Cathay Pacific bound for HKG originating from Melbourne, terminating in BC by way of ADL, I sit down to listen to a young Aussie expert on salmon breeding who is going back to work in Vancouver, he says HKG is under some kind of lockdown from a disease alert threat called *SARS*. When I get back, everyone is wearing masks and the city is locked down. All my gigs get cancelled. (I fancied myself as a bit of Mr Gig man in HK, a big fish in a small pond really — with it, tons of socialising, drinking, snorting, but it kept me well in employment), *SARS* was devastating. SARS was a real trip in HK, at least it was mostly contained locally, geographically speaking. HK was locked down and similar to the recent COVID-19 spectacle. Many hk medical professionals were passing away. All my work was cancelled, walking around downtown resembled a WAR ZONE. People were afraid including me. Fear of the unknown! This COVID-19 has gripped the whole world, no escaping this! I feel extremely satisfied to be in Australia during such a Pandemic. HK is so wealthy, look around - Ferrari, Maserati, Tesla's everywhere, high rise residential estates that cost a fortune! The social security is ludricous. Oz has a system of back up for its people, HK Doesn't. Eventually HK bounced back.

As mentioned in HK, you had Citizens, Doctors and Nurses dying from this bloody thing and the prospects didn't look good. The unknown was frightening, and I put my foot down and told my wife and kids *"we are leaving to go back to Oz now!"* 2003 - SARS was across the road in the building visible from our window (Aus it appeared wasn't so affected by SARS). Then Sylvia freaked saying *"we can't go, I couldn't get a job? We can't go"!* That ended that. So I told the kids we are going to Yangshuo a village in SW China without their mother (where we had all been before) but their passports and going home cards had expired, I was furious, finally after taking about AU$10,000 out of our joint account, we make it to Guilin city and onto Yangshuo.

Within the first few days in YS I find the Budizhen International Kung Fu School and chat with George and Peter Gao (the twin sons of our old late great Budizhen GrandMaster Papa Gao),George & Peter had lived in qld Oz & had a larrikin-ish aura. I enroll Julien my son, Nastassja my daughter and myself immediately into the kung fu school. We start training, I'm so into it and discovering *Qi Gong* for the first time. After a few weeks, I sit the kids down in our very cool hotel room with a balcony, and explain to them that I will take them back to HK and school, but I will return here to train, learn and to get fit again. This is what happens and I'm officially separated...

Rehab Hospital continued...

So back in he rehab hospital I have no family visits, just Li Yin's daily up-vibe appearance, sometimes my ex comes, and girlfriend and the ex are standing at the end of my bed, not a good look and very uncomfortable. Then my ex starts telling the medical team about my home set-up in Mang Kung Uk, Clearwater Bay a three storey house so the medical team won't let me go home unless I move into a single floor flat with no stairs and the ex is supporting this. I am furious but can't do anything really as I don't speak fluent Chinese. Li Yin is a Mainlander lacking Canto skills thus lessening her status to the locals and I don't understand the system, even though I am a HK citizen PR holder.

I am told I won't be able to play guitar for a while, meaning no income. Ron, my best student brings in his Gibson 175 guitar, I assume I'm gonna play it, I can't keep my left hand from dropping off the neck, I'm fucked. Then I really start to worry as I have no insurance, although hkg does have unemployment payments and a pension that I am slated to receive, the amount hardly covers my rent and daily hospital bills. Apparently I am not "eligible" for the unemployment support but am for the disabled pension, which is less. With complete frustration mainly due to language restrictions with the social department, I have to settle on the pension about hkd $2,000 a month / aud $100 a week. My rent is $8,000 a month, I am told to move into a rat room to save money, no thought is given to my business and future, "Go back to Australia" I am told. Would love to hear Centrelink here in Oz trying to say that to immigrants! "Go back Ceylon / India, go back China" etc.!!!:)

Li Yin helps out tremendously. Thank you Li Yinaaaaaaaaaaaaaa

The Hong Kong hospitals are overseen by the ACHS (Australian Council on Healthcare Standards), and on one particular morning the nurses approach me by asking, *"Are you Australian?"* *"Yes!"* I reply, *"OK we have examiners coming today, please say good things to them"*. Sure enough they came 3 aussie nurses/examiners & I said, *"This is what happens to Ageing Asian Aussie RockStars"* and waved around like a *spazzo*...we all laughed. It was nice to meet them and have a chat. The politics of the ward between the nurses and patients got a bit ugly at times in rehab, we are all still in nappies and trying to go to the toilet was always problematic — we are not allowed to go unless accompanied by a nurse.

One day, General is screaming *"aussie, aussie!!!* I raised my hand from across the room and said, *"ngoh hai aussie, lei jo matye a?"* - I'm an Aussie, what's up?

I soon learnt that *"aus si"* means "I need to take a shit" *"si"* = shit AND *"or liu"* = is need a piss. These came in handy sometimes.

I learnt a lot of Canto and I still remember the female nurse who I affectionately named *Gorilla* teaching me:

naan = eyes, *yi jai* = ears, *bei* = nose, *koh* = mouth.

Me and Raymond

Raymond, the young chap in bed opposite me in the rehab ward and I were both perving on the nurses, as we had some very fine specimens there when I arrived, with a look or nod we knew what each was thinking. The nurses and most hospital staff didn't speak English very well, so I would try my crap Cantonese but I was learning. One day after me unsuccessfully trying to understand what the nurses were saying, Raymond blurts out in perfect English *"They wanna know if you need a shower?"* I said *"So you speak English?"* Turns out he had been educated in Manchester in the UK, ate too much KFC and Coke and had a stroke in his early 40s. After exchanging numbers we texted each other about the aptitudes of each hot nurse. Forming the "Ham Sup Lo's Club" (dirty old men's club). We would be giggling when the poor nurse wearing a G- string would pass by, unaware of what we were up to, it was frigging hilarious and from that time onwards we became the best of friends. If not for our antics, it woulda been hellishly boring. Raymond became my new friend and we had a lot of fun.

When I finally could walk unattended but with a stick down to the loo, the whole ward applauded. It reminded me of both school and the *ANZACS*. Sun Wu Kong (old man from Shek O who resembled Monkey King) was rushed to Eastern Hospital and never came back. I just wanted to get out *ALIVE!!*

Raymond went home for a weekend, we were all starting to walk beginning with a walking stick and in the Ward we would applaud if someone was doing it. I felt like I was in an ANZAC POW camp. I started formulating my escape and recovery, I was a believer of Chinese Kung Fu and medicine, hells bells I had lived in China for 3 years studying Tai Chi, and at the end of that tenure won a GOLD medal at the 2006 International Wu Shu competition HKG. But deep down I knew I needed a Si Fu/Shifu/Master to guide and teach me, I couldn't do it on mAccording to my son Julien who reads and writes Chinese,*"Kung"* is Skill, and *"Fu"* is Man, well this book is for everyone and gender. So fuck that!

My mate Raymond tells me it means *"a consistent spiritual and physical practice"* and then what initiates an individual to "Master" status? "Sudden Awakening about the Skill".

Man has always killed Man, we pray for Peace.

Watching & listening to Pat Cummins Oz cricket captain, he talks about learning the skill. He kung fu master.

Through my determination to learn East Asian Kung Fu, I have managed to recover pretty well from a stroke. Some of the benefits are left side, hemiplegia paralysis recovery, I now walk mostly without a stick, conduct Tai Ji classes and have travelled the world since my stroke. I do have a limp & tense uncoordinated left arm /hand. My balance is optimal and from my Sifu - Pang Sifu - I have learnt how to use my weight effectively through body mechanics/ Tai Chi. It's been a worthwhile journey, one that for me ends up acknowledging western science as a reality, combining occidental and oriental as the way and path forward. Awareness is a key state of being & valuable! I believe I pursued tai chi as it is aninternal art... I felt I couldn't pursue hard kung fu or strenuous core work because of my permenant AF/herat problem, I still manitain this belief, but with the guidance of Pang Sifu, I was able to become aware of my body position/ situational awareness. I thank tai chi practice for this.

Aliens were able to heal sick people in outer space where there is no gravity, especially ones with brain injuries. My theory is, us injured people ought to board Elon Musk/Richard Branson's intergalactic `with Asea water pumped into` us with space Physio Therapists for a quick recovery.

In the old world, research and discovery was just a part of life, we got invented, with a large brain. So large, that we human/aliens were filled up with all the information needed to survive. As we forgot, our brains didn't use all the mass we were engineered for, so now there is brain plasticity, re-wiring because we know we are not utilising it all. Other parts take over defunct parts. But only in training.

Aliens: possibly musicians are the most aware of the alien world. Regaining memories of sound harking back to the early days. I reckon surfers too. They feel it! I love my Holden Commodore - a car that was made in Australia, a love that is part territorial and part because it drives so nice. It is a machine and why do I really love it? Do you love your car? To what extant would you cross restraint for it? Would you beat someone up over it? Us human/aliens are engineering and creating more machines, ones that will resemble us to a degree and quite possibly be the end of "us". They will have their brain wired a certain way, no emotion, how can you love a machine? It's possible we all do, but we got emotional content wired in somehow.

Keep an eye on machines try to observe your interaction with them...am I spending too much time with it? am I totes occupied with it? what is it doing to me? Etc!!! go outside and talk to a plant/animal. Nurture your Mother Earth otherwise she won't be here/ or do kung fu:)

Jesus, Nichiren Daishonin, Sri Yuketswar, Shakyamuni, Muhammad were human/aliens that could recollect and remember roots. If you look at pictures and stories about these remarkable individuals, they are *levitated*, they had the grasp of gravity and told us stories, each one franchising to those that could relate, we chose it. I chose Buddha, Nichiren Daishonin therefore I chant Puja &"Nam Myo Ho Renge Kyo", I relate to it. There are so many options to get better. I have been drinking/smoking for 8 years. Because I enjoy it, however the powerful meds obviously – as Leigh said – sustain me, we gonna die, so I like my lifestyle, still here. But maybe not for long.however boredom sets in & I stop.

In An Alien Spaceship

I have had a Cerebrovascular issue CVA STROKE (Cerebrovascular accident) in HK. I am an *AustrAlien*, as well as a Hong Konger, having served my 7 years in HK and got PR (Permanent Residency). Thanks to the Brits and their foresight and generosity, I abide in hospital at 100hkd a day (about AU$20) and it is partially sponsored by the HK Government (the daily fee normally would be way over 100 bucks a day) and the remainder is mainly taken care of by my g/f (cause even with pr that muthafucka is clocking up each week). I have no family here, nor do they contribute financially, as a dumb fuck ex-pat I have no health insurance. Thankfully HK may be the best place in Asia to suffer a stroke. The Doctors and Nurses are magnificent, I say that avoiding all politics in the wards that I encounter later. Whatsoever, some kind of inbuilt mechanism of positivity exists within. I assume all will be well, I joke and cajole, but if it were not for Lyz daily visits, I would have sunk and drowned.

To this day I still don't really understand what has happened, too overwhelming, I wallow in a stroke world of fog and bizarre speech & thoughts. I have grattitude. I feel like I'm floating in a surreal world. I slip into silly childish speech patterns and sounds all the time, but only with people I know real well, like Bellisa, Mum, Li Yin, Chris, Steve, Peter and my support workers - very *mongtard* speech. It is a combination of Aussie & HK bogan- ism sounds & dumb expressions (all *TH* become *F*) and HK english has reinvented itself through strange memories. In fact, I get off on it. In addition to all the *TH's* becoming *F*, there are *R's* becoming *L & vice versa*. And opposingly, *TH* in words like "the, that and them" become *De, Dat, Dem* and Is inverts to *si* ....ie: *Dat si de one*. I need to mull it over in my head to make sure I have altered all the letters correctly. For example: "I Very Sorry, I'm OK Thanks" becomes *Y belly solly, Y wokay fanks*. It's a brain exercise, that makes it 'work' a workout. Honestly the crap Bellisa has to put up with...I also feel/know that eventually we will all be taken by Alien

Spaceship, lucky ones if you can say lucky come back/ I came back to write this this is my destiny xxx.

At the time I don't really think about myself. I have developed a sort of assumption that all will be well. However it doesn't really conclude to this for this dreamer - now nearly ten years after I cannot get out into my workforce, it is permanent. I am fucked for life! Unlike my guitar hero Pat Martino who woke up after a brain operation for the arteriovenous malformation (AVM) causing his siezures If the AVM is in the brain and ruptures, it can cause bleeding in the brain (hemorrhage), stroke or brain damage. The cause of AVMs is not clear. They're rarely passed down among families. Once diagnosed, a brain AVM can often be treated successfully to prevent or reduce the risk of complications. Pat couldn't remember anything, looking at his parents standing beside him, "Who are you?" How to play guitar etc. Similar to the Korean lady who couldn't remember where the local shopping centre was and a host more with this deficiency. I awoke to a dead left sided arm and leg(dead meat) that wouldn't move and that I could barely feel, it was like a butcher had sewn some piece of meat to my torso... no going down the beach like Geoff Dyer or Martin, I was crippled, *Fucked!* Pat obviously had movement but couldn't remember how or what to play, I had the mental cognitive functions but I couldn't do it, still can't. Instead of Dustin Hoffman trapped in a woman's body as a bloke, I was trapped in a body that wouldn't move... Ga La Wor! I conjure a spectacle that I had actually been taken away in an alien spaceship, then returned to earth. Its amazing what you can convince yourself of...

Notable musoz who had also been space lifted returned as strokers include – Keith Jarrett, Dennis Chambers, Barry Harris, Oscar Peterson, Tommy Ho, Oliver Smith. Of course many had never returned, staying in space.

Katoomba November 2019

It is a trip not being able to contribute to *the city of the arts, Blue Mountains.*when I lived in Katoomba pre stroke I was like a poc guy king up here 30 years ago, having come off the road with top Aussie bands *Eurogliders, Ian Moss Band, Matt Finish*, then securing Head of guitar department at the *Australian Institute of Music.*

Now in a bit of a shell of a body with brain damage Spasticity and left side paralysis, meaning no guitar playing. I wanted to prove the medical wrong about this, but they are proving right. I'm wrong! A GA LA WOR. It reminds me of Santana's "Game of Love", there are no winners in this stroke game. Ga La!

FB: Macau 20?

...Oh my god, being the bandleader for a jazz band at the Venetian Casino, Macau. A Fucking Six month Nightmare! That's it before they send out killers to silence me Ga La!...

Pauline Murray, author of "*A Brush with Stroke*" writes in her chapter - Understanding Stroke –"...Every Stroke is different. Whether you had a stroke or are caring for someone who has had a stroke, it helps to understand why strokes can be so different. It has been estimated that in 2009 some 50,000 people in Australia will have had a Stroke. One third of that number will be left with a degree of disability, from mild to severe. It is important to understand the nature of the disability and how it will impact on your future: at home, in the community and at work."

The Brain At Work

To understand Stroke, it helps to understand a little of how the brain functions. This will help to explain why no two strokes are the same. The brain has zones or areas that are purpose-designed and not only allow us to see and hear, but to also make sense of what we see and hear. While other areas allow us to move and keep our balance and make reasoned judgements. The book continues with real stuff, I recommend it.

Often I think had I had my stroke in Oz followed the pragmatic oz science related recovery methology, combined with 1st nations people medicinal, spiritual ways, that I may have recovered fully. I just told Bell that, Asians moved to western countries and became *"Westernised"*, I moved to Asia and became *"Asianised"* as did my HK western buddies.

FB: Mexico 1976

...Arriving with Mum and Eddy into Palenque, the Yucatan, Mexico, was further enhanced with the view of Mayan ruins, and hopes of consuming purple mushrooms, in these days it was always a pleasure to get up early and go exploring. Once near Lake Atitlan in Guatemala, I got up so early, grabbed my guitar and picks ran out of the van to explore, only upon returning finding it rocking up and down, so with my 5 cent avocadoes & guitar picks I scooped the flesh out & waited for the *frenzy* to subside before tapping on the van door....

I'm listening to an ancient Egyptian chant on youtube titled "A Ku Dua". It reminds me of a space song with the planets circling going about their business, there is a candle burning with an orange background..... *"Now I'm the king of the swingers, oh the jungles VIP, I've reached the top and had to stop and that's what'sa bothering me.*

RECOVERY

Recovery is tied in with age, health condition, attitude, hard work and focus. Engage with community. Try to develop a positive attitude.

My own recovery - I can walk (with limp), deal with stairs (with railing), and blessedly use my brain to problem solve, drive, - began with determinedly pursuing physio/rehab, kung fu & not being lazy. I was committed. Recovery is not a miracle.

Mick was in a horrific car accident, but got himself back to playing drums. I heard him recently in the Baby Animals & it was awesome!

Kung fu stories...

MY KUNG FU ~ ONE / PRE-STROKE

My *kung fu* around the 1970's and 80's was playing Guitar. I studied and practiced guitar hard for years.[SEP] Other Kung Fu'z were - Surfing / Cycling / Skiing / Study / Daydreaming / Mexico /travelling. When I say 'My Kung Fu' I mean my skills, activity I focussed on with passion and developed over a period of time. Not kung fu fighting. But an engagement. With devotion & passion, this is what we all need to pull ourselves out of the ruts – could be gardening, praying, meditating, doing, being. Chop, chop fai deea, as said by Bellisa.

My Chinese Martial ARTS Kung Fu journey and training began in 1975 in high school, clearly tv shows like Kung Fu. Marine Boy, Astro Boy, Samurai & the Phantom Agents coming from Japan with their jap martial arts influenced big time! I bought & studied Mas Oyama's kyokoshinkai karate books, after seeing Lo Wei's 'Five Fingers of Death' I began training out the back, stump fisting and katas & with Felizardo – recently arrived from Manila/replicating everyone's Hero Bruce Lee to a T. Once I saw Bruce Lee's films I flipped and became a devout Chinese kung fu follower.

Real tuition kicked in in November 1979, when I first arrived in Hong Kong. Like most kids born around my time of 1960. We were blown away by Bruce Lee. So I took myself over to Kowloon Tong and stood outside Bruce Lee's house freaking, with an imagination gone wild, I decided to pursue *Wing Chun Kung Fu* although I loved *Tong Long kuen/quan* – (Praying Mantis boxing*)*.

After walking up and down Nathan Rd, Kowloon exploring, I settled on a sign in ultra populated Mongkok with a dark stairway that read "*Po Kin Wah's Ving Tsun Athletic Association.*" I ran up the stairs, met Po Kin Wah Sifu and his Si Hing and it was agreed I would join and start immediately. At this time I was living in Yung Shue Wan, Lamma Island - located behind HK Island, across from Aberdeen, (a 45 mins ferry ride from Central) and had my first professional gig thanks to Dale Wilson - a 5 evening a week gig playing solo guitar in posh *Marin Ushka* restaurant, Lan Kwai Fong. So I was able to get over to Mongkok for training before my gig most days. I came to view Ving Tsun as a science, there was force, yielding, deflecting, sudden forces of power, *Tan Sao, Bong Sau, Chi Sao*. Love Wing Chun, still practice today.

It was all fascinating and I still pretty much remember the 3 forms: *Siu Nam Tao, Chum Kiu and Biu Tse.*

Si Hing (senior) was a skinny guy who had real power, often I would spar with Sifu only to come out with a red chest and often flying through the air backwards because Chi Sao - sticking hands between 2 people - is like a game of feeling while your arms are interlocked and if you feel an opening you slap or punch through; use Bong Sau or some other to deflect it if you can, otherwise you get hit or pushed over. It's fun when you don't take it too seriously. Chi Sao is the beginning & introduction to sparring. Sifu often pitted me against another student. A very muscly looking HK policeman, he always won btw. I felt like I was living in a kung fu dream movie through all of this, it was truly amazing. Interestingly with a foundation in Wing Chun, which emphasises straightline centre focus & weight more on back foot. My future Tai Chi training would introduce circular and flowing weight awareness & deflection. Quite the opposite of Wing Tsun training. But ultimately similar when you Master:)

Si (seated)

I had applied to go to *Berklee College of Music* in Boston USA, and was accepted. Meanwhile, Dad was living in Paris. The time was coming to leave hkg and girlfriend (Sylvia) - On my last day at Ving Tsun, Sifu put me up against mister Policeman however this time I was able to overcome him. I won! It was an amazing feeling. With Sifu Po Kin Wah, I learnt the 3 forms *Some Mok Yan Jong* and *Chi Sao*.

BRUCE LEE

The closest I ever got to Bruce Lee was standing outside his house on Cumberland St in Kowloon Tong, at age 19 walking on his footsteps then meeting Shih Kien- *Mr Han* in *Enter the Drago*n at Cafe do Brasil in Ocean

Terminal Tsim Sha Tsui. Then many years later going to the Bruce Lee exhibition at Sha Tin Museum, Hong Kong, seeing the actual yellow suit he wore on "Game of Death". Also meeting and working for Jon Benn the mafia boss in "Way of the Dragon", by playing in his bar located in Mid-Levels *Bruce Lee Cafe* for two years (where I played with the beautiful charismatic Elaine Liu in duo).

Basically I thought Bruce Lee was a talented prick, a typical arrogant spoilt little HK fucker in which it all began because he was Lee Hoi Chuen's son and Gwai Jai (half Chinese, half Western) with a childhood of starring in local hk movies & a family with money. He basically was the epitome of typical HK forces of east and west coming together at the right time and creation. Just like Tai Ji.

He could sweet-talk - in North American jive/ knew the Canto jive and vulgar slang, lay on Charm and dance around with a cha-cha. Jeet Kune Do his kung fu style is a style of MMA coming together with the elements at the right time.

Nonetheless, as I have begun this chapter on a negative note, the truth for me to say, is that may be my own internal problem. On a positive note, Bruce Lee certainly was a talented, clever and creative individual. He would have been accepted into Raymond/ Guy's Ham Sup lo Club, momantai no problem!

> "Also the mystical mind training promotes not the promised internal power but psychological constipation."
> - Bruce Lee.

ENTER THE DRAGON is possibly Bruce Lee's most popular movie. Being his highest earning movie, It certainly was the one that grabbed me....the similarities to James Bond 007 flicks are many. Opens up with shots of HK, like 007 *You Only Live Twice*, introduces a dude who has an uncanny resemblance to 007 (John Saxon- Sean Connery)

Brings in an exotic oriental flavour and sex a la orient. Asian language and etiquette. 007 Japan, Enter HK Chinese. In *You Only Live Twice(released 1st)* when the Japanese chick turns up at the Sumo match with the big oval eyes, I was smitten! And she drove a fast sports car, with ease and exuberance. Awesome chick. "Fletcher" had lived in Japan for 28 years (about the time I lived in HK) and is killed as he is about to confess to 007 the power behind the enemy, in true *Fist of Fury* style 007 smashes the Japanese rice paper walls, runs out into the dark garden and terminates the killer, very much like when Bruce Lee knocks off Robert Baker. The stories weren't very original, copying western hits blended with wuxia stories.

Bruce Lee's jumpsuit from the movie "The Game of Death" (Hong Kong Heritage Museum in Sha Tin)

FB: USA 1980

...I loved being in the USA. I had seen and spent considerable time there as a 16yr old. The US had an energy. At age 20 and arriving in NYC for the first time after an emotional flight leaving my girlfriend Sylvia and Mum in HK, I'm thinking of staying over here in *The Big Apple* before I hop on the greyhound bus up to Boston, but the yellow cab driver won't let me, he's taking me straight to *Port Authority* bus station to get on that bus, *"Don't talk to no-one, it's dangerous out there"*. I feel like I'm in a trip movie. Some time passes after living and studying in Boston then visiting Paris and London, living back in HK. I wouldn't get back to training kung fu until I moved back to Sydney in 1981 where I pursued: *Yau Kung Mun, Choy Lay Fut, Kickboxing* and then *Wu Shu "Long Fist" Chang Quan* in 1983.... Chang Quan "Long Fist" (Wu Shu) - Chinese Youth League with Teacher Fong Lee

It was with Teacher Fong Lee of the Sydney Chinese Youth League Aus. that I committed. Appreciative of the graceful and elegant Wu Shu forms that were employed by mainland China in competition and movies like *"Shaolin"*, I kept at it weekends and trained with fellow student William. Fong was an unusual character in so much as he had taught himself all the forms and moves from little books one could buy on Dixon St, Chinatown. Eventually we all flocked there to buy them. Teacher Fong Lee was from China but had a very *Australian* feel. Nothing fazed him, I liked him a lot. Eventually he was featured on the front cover of Australian Martial Arts magazine *Blitz* in 2006. My tenure with the Chinese Youth League phased out as I tenaciously climbed the Sydney music scene to become a fairly in demand guitarist, doing session work and touring. Finally in the pop group

Eurogliders for three years and later in the *Ian Moss Band* as a member - All *Kung Fu* training stopped.

It wasn't until a near burnout stage at age 43 while based in HK and holidaying in Yangshuo (YS) south western China with my kids did I begin training and learning again. In 2003 I based myself in YS China, which broke up the family. The ignorance and avoidance toward me from my children has ensued from that point in time. Clearly they were very emotionally affected. Sometimes ya gotta do what ya gotta do. To survive may be better than dead. I found the BudiZhen School in YS fascinating as I participated in Papa's *Qi Gong*. I was also into the Tai Chi, but wouldn't really devote wholly to it until I moved to Shenzhen (SZ) a year later following Chen style tai ji.

My Hypothetical

Tai Chi is a martial art that came to its practitioners through a remembrance of outer space. It is a space dance where there is no gravity. Similar to being high on some mind alterant, the kung fu man experiences a paradigm shift in his martial practice and becomes at one with the Alien Masters.

Check this out my hero if he not in space den where he?

https://www.youtube.com/watch?v=GaoAMjEh8g

Kung Fu. In Chinese, it is generally known as **kung fu/kungfu/gung fu** - In Canto/ **gongfu** - In Mando (/ˌkʊŋ ˈfuː/; 功夫, Pinyin: **gōngfu**) and refers to

> A practice that requires patience, energy and time to complete. In its original meaning, kung fu can refer to any discipline or skill achieved through hard work and practice, not necessarily martial arts. The Chinese literal equivalent of "Chinese martial art" would be 中國武術 ZhōngGuó Wǔshù. (Zhongguo meaning China).the Chinese martial arts, also called Wushu and Quanfa. In China, it refers to any study, learning or practise.

You too can be a kung fu lord.

Kung Fu actually means skill, a two syllable word exported & popularised by Hong Kong cinema, unfortunately for the Chinese race it was not invented in China. *Chinese Martial Arts* roots are in human war machines that one can discover in all armies from the Greeks, Romans, Russians, the Huns etc. They all had violent Kung Fu/combat. It's not like it was invented in China, we can say the Chinese systemised their combat combos to an attractive looking dance routine. Vikings had berserkers, probz totes unpredictable & improvised it probz wasnt a good look.

The Hong Kongers were clever and able to brand 'kung fu' through their movies, nearly patenting it, the commercialisation, fraud, different interpretations & promotions, ownership branded are a bit sickening. A deeper look reveals other worldly versions...

World Kung Fu's

USSR - *Systema, Sambo*

India - *Kalari Payattu, Mahabharata, Shastar Vidiya*

Greece – *Pankration*

Middle East - *Silat, Sumerian Boxing, Tahtib, Wrestling*

Israel - *Krav Maga*

Brasil - *Capoeira, Brazilian Ju Jitsu*

Africa - *Laamb, Stick Fighting*

Australia – *Coreeda Aboriginal martial arts, MDTA - Modern Defence Tactics Australia, another Australian method comes from the 1st Nations people, aboriginals focussing on wrestling and even dance which fascinatingly follows the native oz animals behaviour & moves.*

Europe - *Savate, Glima, HEMA, Fencing, Archery, Wrestling, Boxing.*

Japan - *Aikido, Judo, Karate (originally called 'China fist'), Ju Jutsu Kenpo, Sumo Wrestling, Ninjutsu.*

Korea - *Hapkido, Tae Kwon Do, Tang Soo Do.*

SE Asia, Indonesia, Cambodia, Philippines respectively - *Pencak Silat, Bokator, Lethwei, Arnis, Eskrima, Muay Thai Boxing* (from Thailand - A country never colonised).

UK - *Bare Knuckle Boxing, Western Boxing, Defendu.*

Canada - *Combato, Defendo, Okicitaw*

USA - *Boxing (WBC and WBF), MMA/UFC (Ultimate Fighting Championship) Defendu.*

New Zealand - *Mau Rakai (weapons based skill)* How can I forget our Kiwi brothers- half of the ANZAC treaty (Australian New Zealand Army Corps). The indigenous people of the country, The Maoris are renowned Warriors, their Kung Fu so mighty that the whites were forced to sign treaties, as kids at school, we were introduced and often participated in Maori activities, the poi performance and the Haka.)

China – Wing Chun (Ving Tsun), Pak Mei (white eyebrow), Choy Lay Fut (name of buddhist monk), Hung Kuen(begun by wealthy tea merchant), Tai Ji Quan (yin yang boxing), Pa Gua Quan (8 trigram boxing), Xing Yi Quan, Praying Mantis, Monkey, Dragon, Leopard, Crane, Snake, Tiger, Plum fist styles, Shaolin & Wudang

Public displays/busking:) - Opera and Dance troupes.

Let's not forget the advancement of martial arts for winning and Bodyguard/ Combat, Security work

Finally the deadliest kung fu of all: **THE GUN AND THE BULLET**. Interestingly a small study or observation reveals a strong similarity to internal power *gung fuz*... a sudden sharp explosive power, (*fa jin/fa ging*) catapulting, rotating moving quickly forward, the bullet in a straight line, rotating circularly at high speed (possibly the most effective punch).

As Buddhist philosophy along with Taoism matured and fused in China. Possibly a peace and awareness began to pervade Chinese Society, culminating in a less *"martial"* approach to kung fu and a more thoughtful awareness of the health benefits utilising it more as an exercise. Besides the martial aspect, we have combined the spiritual and passion, religious and medical advancements thus influencing and co-existing with body movement kung fu. Many kung fu artists became Doctors – being able to treat afflicted patrons.

The current view on Chinese Martial Arts seems to sit with either:

1. Kung Fu for *Health, Longevity & exercise*

2. Kung Fu for *Self-Defense*

3. Kung Fu for *Fighting/combat - Offense.*

Whichever, **all** require "Attitude"!

~ Kalaripayattu ~ Mother of Kung Fu!

"Kalaripayattu and Shastar Vidiya" (Indian military fighting styles) from India are in my opinion the precursors to Chinese Kung Fu as we know it. Check them out. It is said *Boddhidharma* arrived at Shaolin Temple (supposedly the birthplace of Chinese Kung Fu) from India, he was a *Kalaripayattu* dude, agility and flexibility being its key components linking it to Yoga, which I always believed was a training discipline for the incredible Indian warriors. Most new thought etc. in the early days arrived in China from India.

If you dig into Chinese culture, a tremendous likeness and linkage reveals itself between the two countries. Indian culture has greatly influenced Chinese. The adaptable Chinese were able to assimilate and make it theirs. I always believed Yoga was a means to train and ready the military units of India, now it is considered a health practice, much like most of the Mainland's Kung Fu.

The downfall of Asian martial arts is they were unable to keep up with science. Subtracting the motion of 'Core' exercise and relying on a static technique steeped in hoo ha, will not stack up against a fit animal in defence or offence. Unfortunately.

I have just blown the myth. U may go now! Are we there yet?

The Egyptian human aliens knew many secrets (manipulating gravity & energy). This ancient knowledge traversed east from Egypt (known as *Aku*) to India (known as *Prana*) mentioned above, until in China they called it *Qi-Chi* or internal energy. The Chinese were very observant, as all human aliens yearned for their mother land we all took to looking upwards, praying, building monuments all pointing to space and called it *God*. The Chinese observed the circles and roundness in the sky - planets, motions and concluded as did their inventors. Incorporating it into social dances resulting in kung fu forms.

Experimenting with circular (like scientists) they found more power evolves out of circular rather than straight (circular & straight a drill or gun – most powerful combination). Supplementing other physics (knowledge of nature) with observance of animals (snake/tiger/crane/leopard/dragon) the doped out Chinese martial artists developed their own kung fu, these matured into systems over time and with the explosive arrival of *Hong Kong kung fu* movies. Bruce Lee influenced westerners, like me, were "hooked". Captivating me so much so that I married a Hong Kong girl and went over there to live and became a HKG citizen, studied *kung fu* for yonks! So the myth of Chinese *kung fu* is broken, It is anyone's Kung Fu.

I believe **Kung Fu**

belongs to **Everyone**. Thank you.

bushfires OZ 2019

I wanna be a man, man-cub the jungles vip, ive reached the top and had to stop, thats whats sa bothering me, I wanna be a man cub and stroll right into town, now gimme the secret of Mans' great power so I can make fire, I dunno how to make fire". Jungle book.

Ravi Shankar – Ravi = Sun, Australian Bushfires 2019 ~ 2020 -

these were scary especially around the blue mountains, NSW and beyond were terribly affected, then came the floods – unbelievable.

MY KUNG FU~TWO/POST STROKE 2015

Stroked & Seeking recovery in Kung Fu Activity

..."I have gone kung fu crazy! I'm seeking every possible avenue and training to recover"...

I am still based in HK, being supported by LY, hoping to recover and get back to work. Fortunately I can now walk a bit, move my left paralysed side. In Hong Kong there are ample opportunities to follow Chinese kung fu. I am possibly in the kung fu centre of the world. I signed up to so many, eventually discovering it was too much.

Dragging Li Yin to Kowloon Park most Sundays to see the live Kung Fu demonstrations in Statue Square, I witnessed Zhaobao Tai Chi for the first time with Sifu Kwan Wing Kwong and at the end of his performance, he asked everyone to join him. I jumped in & found the moves engaging and wanted to do more, I introduced myself to him and he put me onto his top student, Dennis - an ex-cop — who ran classes of his *Modern Method* with Harry Lok. I joined the Modern Method in Kowloon Bay every Saturday...his classes combined self defense with *Tae Kwon Do* and I enjoyed it, but I was hoping to get a more Tai Chi vibe, with further research I found Master Pang Sifu through his book *Fa Ging Zhaobao Tai Chi (King Tai Chi)* in HK Commercial bookstore. The martial arts word *King* in Canto is really pronounced *Ging, as in fa ging:)* which in Mando is *Fa Jin(internal power)*.

Jin or ging is internal explosive power. Not king and queen like, or some magical mystical item.It is fired out of the body through the skeletal rails through a combination of body mechanics and the waist muscle – the kua. Pure physics.

Anyway we arranged to meet at HK library. Pang is polite, speaks English, went to UNSW is Australian also, stocky and steadily built. He used to be a HK high school teacher and loves physics, he is going on about body mechanics in true kung fu, and demonstrates...asking me to give him my arm. With arm upon arm, he sinks his weight unexpectedly, his COG (centre of gravity) dropping on me is overwhelming. His power is massive(assisted by his weight and muscle) I felt faint and I was totally gone, thought I was gonna have another blooming stroke, I was totally overcome by his power of just sinking forcing me to the ground like I collapsed.

I was intrigued, and signed up after I also witnessed the 12 move form and got his book. Sifu allowed me to join 2-3 classes a week even if I was broke. He is a good man, we connect real well. I go to HK library down the road every Tuesday evening and to Kowloon Park every Saturday to join his classes.

King Tai Chi Fa Jin Research Centre HONG KONG/CHINA. Head - Master William Pang.

After searching for a Hong Kong Sifu, to aid me in stroke recovery, continue my passion & engagement in kung fu practice and study, as well as guide me, and spending good time training with Yim Sifu in his *Tai Chi Gong*, and Dennis (ex-police) *Modern Method &* Missy Master Lily Kwok *Chen Xiao Wang Tai Chi HK*. Visiting renowned hk author C.S.Tang, strolling around in commercial printer bookshop thus finding Master Pang's 'Mechanics of Tai Chi - Zhao Bao style' with website and email.

I needed to reduce my engagements with so many kung fuz to be able to focus on one.

I contact Master Pang Hon Keung and we meet at the library, where he installed the "gyroscope" that was one hell of an installation! So after a discussion about his teaching career and students and my lack of finances, it was agreed that I would start immediately on Tuesdays at the library — suited me as at that time I was living across the road in Moreton Terrace, in a crap room, Saturdays in Kowloon Park. I still had a painful issue with my left shoulder and decided with some encouragement from my physio Jackson to stop tai chi gong classes that involved raising hand and arms to the heaven plus a stick routine that was killing me. My King Tai Chi *Si Hings* (senior brothers- a respectable respect) are Dr. Chu, KC, Tim, William, KL, Anthony Ma, Patrick, Steve Sing and Uncle Wah who dates back to being a school student of Sifu when he was a high school teacher, all have some pretty deep foundations in Tai Chi/ Kung Fu. It's easy to complain about things in hkg. My initial understanding through the website was that there was a Fa Jin Research Centre of which I then envisioned daily trips to this particular place. But alas, HK property is scarce and ridiculously expensive, so everything is "virtual". We meet & train in public spaces. We focus on 12 moves, from the 12 move set, there is a 75 set too, and marbling games – trying to move one out of a position, both using internal fa ging & each move from the 12 set.

Pang Sifu, is a disciple of Master Xi Chung-Sui & considers himself a Tai Chi theorist, he is not a fighter military man. Indeed he's a gentle soul, passionate about Tai Chi and real power in Kung Fu. Try to move him outside a circle and you would be hard pushed, come at him with a flying punch or kick and I don't know what he'd do. He does the form eloquently with sudden powerful explosive physical bursts. Pang doesn't talk in dilly dally Taoist speech, it is sensible direct scientific talk. As with all the training I have done to date in China/HK, there is no focus on aggressive connections, no *tui shou*, grappling or sparring. Indeed I've come to realise we are seeking a peaceful, meditative focussed intent meditation. To expand ourselves individually, like true spiritual fulfillment. Clearly at my stage with disability, I am pursuing the health factor of kung fu.

Later in Australia, I will come to realize after all these years I have not really inherited a system of self defense and I will ask myself defense questions with researched answers, settling mainly on my kung fu history and Defendu. Direct nasty *modern tactics* for survival. As I continue my research for this book, I am beginning to see what I would do. It would be deadly direct and nasty offensive *modern tactics. Your core needs to be strong.*

My fellow students and Si Hings...

KL's background is in Wudang, and if you research that it seems a Hong Kong guy named Cheng Ting Hun created this style and the HK Tai Chi Association. Continued by Cheng Kam Yan - his son. KL is good. William and I have sparred in Ving Stun Chi Sao. He is good also, like a gentle giant. Uncle Wa must weigh 40 kg's looks like a kid but he's got some power and seems to know most of the 75.

By the way, in this school, knowing the sets/form is meaningless, it's the correct execution of each move and its correlated Jin that counts and I must say even though I am a foreigner and HK citizen, there IS a bit of smirking and general *hoo ha* by the locals at me, but on the other hand I have turned up at parks in HK and mainland China and someone there has taken it upon themselves to teach me something, all in the good, Xie xie Se Sifu SZ.

As I have gone kung fu crazy, I'm seeking every possible avenue and training to recover. My aim is to recover and eventually walk, act physically like a Tai Chi dude. This actually happens as I walk and climb stairs, pathways with arms placed in front for protection – falls -collisions, the imaginary balancing chi ball between my hands, even to this day. It stabilises me, and continual awareness of my weight placement and unlocking joints, like knees arms – I call it *YI GONG* (mind skill).My Tai Ji kung fu is instilled in me, for all my actions. My Yi Gong is central to my recovery and attitude, perhaps you could develop your own Yi Gong…? Sometimes I feel like the robot in lost in space, at the sense of danger my arms go up and wave in defense of imminent danger:)

The Pavilion in Kowloon Park where we train is full of other Sifus (masters) teaching. *Tai Chi Chen, Yang style, Yi Quan.* Lots of styles and activity, it's interesting and I commit full-time to Pangs classes for a bit over a year.

Where I lived with Li Yin, buses could be caught to get anywhere, so this is how this book started, with me sitting on the buses stuck in traffic writing, somewhat like a diary jotting down observations and thoughts.

I would get the bus down the library that travelled down the eastern corridor (same route as when I was transported from one hospital to the other). Sitting on the top deck with brilliant views over to Kowloon across the harbour, and massive concrete residences and offices on the left as we cruised down reclaimed land totes stunning!. Turning off then passing through the village feel of *Tin Hau*, I would hop off a few stops down at the library/ victoria park stop, run to the back of the library near Deli France and dive into Pang Sifu's world of body mechanics and *Zhaobao* style tai chi kung fu.

Every Saturday it was Kowloon Park at the pavilion where quite a few other kung fu masters met their students to train. Kowloon Park is on the other side of the harbour, I would take the tunnel bus, pull out my computer and write for the long journey. In the tunnel I remembered being born. *Are we there yet?* It was in K park that I witnessed **Yi Quan** every single Saturday as our own school had Dr. Chu, a renowned HK physician and senior in our ranks. He had started his kung fu in the tradition of Yi Quan along with the Yi Quan Sifu (Sifu/master Bo) who was there every Saturday. So Dr. Chu transmitted a lot of his ideas with an underlying Yi Quan- ness. Yi Quan is way cool.

Living at Li Yin's single floor flat *I UniQ* in Shaukeiwan enabled me to go to physio twice a week, run around searching for kung fu, as well as meet John who inducted me into his world of Nichiren Buddhism, which I later embraced.

Si hings cont'- KC is a bit of a grumpy older bloke, I think he thinks I'm a bit of a joke, but assuming is wrong. Most Hong Kongers have a bit of an ego and are more than willing to prove themselves, whether it be a game, spending money/buying the most shit, showing off, but I do remember a time when I was with Zhang in Donghu Gongyuan (park) SZ, and a hkg bloke came up to me (I was normal then) and he wanted to play Chi Sao as he had heard I had played Wing Chun. So we engaged and his attitude and strength surprised me for a "friendly'", same thing happened at the Pavilion the other Saturday, and I'm disabled, I thought that guy was a bit over the top, and I felt like I wanted to drop him but could not. KC has extensive background in Yang Tai Ji. His master of many years recently passed on. KC patiently spends time with me on foundation - placement of feet and I respect him. Anthony is also Canadian, so we are able to discuss many things in English, he has helped me better understand my posture and awareness of my tailgate.

A Sing looks very young to me, and is the "natural", watching his moves makes me think he's "got it", sometimes reminds of skiing or gliding on ice. The Zhaobao special skill of walking, incredibly everything is circular even utilising half circles. Small frame as opposed to the Chen Tai Ji large frame. I admire both, but for the moment I prefer the small frame as I contend with my disability.

The smaller hand/arm movements and stances of Zhaobao seemed more appropriate for me. I discovered that Pang Sifu focuses heavily on Fa Jin mechanics, as he had worked out the code of Fa Jin in a scientific way with Physics, Bio Mechanics, Momentum Theory as a science. In the beginning and still today we work on our Fa Jin (internal power) skills/strength. As Sifu studied biology and graduated from both HKU and UNSW, science had been an area of gratitude and fascination for him. He prefers to call himself a Tai-Chi theorist. We haven't done any Tui Shou/Push Hands/ Sparring, we avoid violence. We play strength games using *"Marbling"* trying to outdo each other by pushing one over the line, always aware of our pillar, brake and posture, we use our pelvis positioning and pelvis waist muscle *(Kua). The kua is the secret to power.*

The waist contracts then elastically expands to release a *Jin* which travels along the skeletal system to be fired out to where one's mind let's it. The kua movement also massages our lymph system. Exiting a tremendous force out of the body called *Fa Jin* in Mando or *Fa King* in Canto (pronounced far-ging) hence the name of our school King Tai Chi.

As my left side is still not operating properly, it is difficult for me to conduct these subtle moves. At times I have wanted to quit but I keep going along, like the scene in *The Jungle Book...*

> *"I dunno, well what cha wanna do? I dunno what cha wanna do?"* Go do Kung Fu.

In the beginning I was not searching for Fa Jin skills but as Sifu explained we use a muscle (waist muscle) that we hardly ever use, it also massages the internal organs and lymphatic system, plus one's kung fu is greatly enhanced. The secret is in the waist. With all this and a visual style that is subtle with Yin Yang, what is there not to like?! In addition, a very important issue was the English language skills of Pang and other members of school. I think I had had it with trying to learn something in Chinese(I have basic Chinese language skills). So after about 8 months I was able to let go of all the others *Chen Xiao Wang, Modern Method, Yim's Tai Chi Gong & focus solely on King Tai Chi.*

We also have a website, *kingtaichi.org*, and prospective students can opt for distance learning via the site. Sifu teaches a "12 move set", the 1st move like "opening" Sifu seems to refer to as the 1st Jin. In fact each move is a Jin, so there is absolutely no "dancing" in his instruction. I still cannot execute this 1st Jin properly, and if you can't do the 1st Jin then learning "12" or "72" doesn't mean anything, just someone moving, with no substance, nothing, more like a dance – whatever turns you on I guess. Indeed Sifu has HK locals, mainlanders (he can speak Mando), and overseas students, we train in the Tai Chi land of Hong Kong, the pavilion at Kowloon Park as Sifu operates in hkg, and admits to be more of a Tai Chi theorist, than fighter.

https://www.youtube.com/watch?v=Cu8ZwL0cbNY&t=45s

I have worried about the situation for Sifu if someone would challenge him to fight (not uncommon in HK), his response is to already have an answer in mind for such situations and take photos to pursue legal action. The art of fighting without fighting?:)My Wing Chun master advised me to run away as fast as possible, if a fight arose:)

Following are some excerpts from interviews I have done with our students...

Senior Doctor Chu Yi Si.

Dr. Chu began his studies as a Chinese medical practitioner specialising in Skeletal/bones. His martial arts started with Yi Quan, along with Sifu Bo at the Saturday Pavilion. Together they studied with Master Yip Hai-Sing learning all of Yi Quan. Yi Quan is way cool, the student explained to me

> *"we use our mind to move and we are totally aware of our movement inclusive of attack and defense".*

As I have peaked at Bo's students and exercises, I couldn't help notice the way they rise and curve their arms, as if carrying a big fitness ball and suddenly a "snap" or what I assume is a type of Fa Jin power to fire off the opponent. I ask Dr. Chu about this and he said it is a Fa gin power...created by the back/spine with Dantian, which transmits power. The mechanical working as far as action is concerned is different from our Zhaobao mechanics but the concept is the same.

Dr. Chu met Pang Sifu three years ago and began following him. As Pang's clear succinct instructions offered have basically attracted all the locals in school and also it seems Sifu's 2 books, based on the mechanics of Fa Jin have steered prospective students his way.

Dr. Chu is also recognised as a Qi Gong master, and along with William have advised me not to practise my Budizhen Qi Gong - possibly also known as " Iron Shirt Qi Gong" as it is too martially oriented for someone like me. We have done Ba Duan Jin, and some exercises, swinging hands/arms. At the end of a session we always sing and do the last *zha yi* into a *zhang zhuang*, standing tree meditation pose and Sifu sings his song.

William has background in Wing Chun, he is the big lovable dangerous bear.

Patrick is a senior who always wins the marbling & is hilariously funny. We are always laughing at the cha chaan teng (tea snack restaurant) after training.

A new song we have written with lyrics by Pang Sifu that he sings in tree standing, that I managed to put together with my top student Ron Ng at home under Sifu's watch with Li Yin singing.

"Me-cha-nic king tai chi jin Hong Kong rooted made it known Yin yang mind mo-mem-tum rise Dan-tian load-ing spiral strength Bare-ly touch-ing force re-bound Hum-ble guy u-ni-ver-se king O-ver o-ver bat-tle life Run-ning run-ning bat-tle life Running, running, peace in mind"

https://soundcloud.com/search?q=liyin%20guy%20leclaire

15th Nov 2015 HK post stroke

Well, that was a day! Was so looking forward to meeting Pang at 4pm at Dai Hok (Chinese University) then a dinner. Got on de wrong bus.

Arm raises are killing my left shoulder — all along I thought I had frozen shoulder/ bursitis or an athletic injury, but it turns out it is *Neuro* - totes brain nerve related. Have you ever seen a map of the nerves of our body? It's incredible. The arm has the Ulnar, Radial and Median nerve pathways. This was my problem, but I didn't know until I got with Lee Cossey and Chris Flowers, Physio's of Move Clinic, Katoomba Australia.

This left arm shoulder pain is still with me. I am currently following physio instructions to re-wire my brain by intensive repetition and build muscle mass. I believe it, as yesterday while playing guitar, I felt my left arm didn't have enough strength to execute, first time I really felt that.

Today I mainly play/ teach 8 pieces Ba Duan Jin Qi Gong & some king tai chi, then carefully doing each move of *Lao Jia* old frame form.

In HK I lasted about 6 months with all these kung fuz – a kung fu a day, then had a bit of a burn out, thinking, *"Jack of all trades, master of none"*, so I just focused on Pang Sifu and right before I left HK in Dec 2015 at our annual dinner awards, I was awarded "Certificate of Recognition Head Coach" and 1st place award in marble power competition.

Pang and I along with KC and Caitlin went on TV to talk about our school, you can find it here at **https://youtu.be/Wie3ZZn5WeE** (part 2 of 2 TV interview starts at the 8min mark)

Here at the annual gala Pang hopes I can give a speech, as I am the only English speaking foreigner. I get up on stage in an attempt to give a speech, looking up I suddenly became overwhelmed and choked up. I stood there unable to speak and cried my eyes out. It was so embarrassing. Am I a man? A kung fu man? The fact that I was awarded and could physically stand in front of these people after all the trauma was too much, uncontrollable crying so embarrassing ga la w or!:)

I fucked it up, Even Jackie Chan says the one thing he's most afraid of are public speeches.

Did I tell you about the time I hung out all night with Jackie Chan? here goes...

...Playing and being a part of Blaine Whittaker's bands was a real pleasure, Australian sax ace (HKer) Blaine is always very professional and a fantastic player, we have done many great gigs. This time we are part of HK star *Michael Wong's Band* gigging in Hangzhou. In the airport luggage collection area, we bump into other top HK musos claiming they are playing with Jackie Chan, anyway we are all hanging out with Michael after our gig jamming at JZ Hangzhou and Michael gets a call from Jackie, so we all pile in a cab and go to JC's place, he is just like in the movies, except I'm only inches from him.

Hanging out with Jackie Chan

Now what is Chinese Kung Fu?

It is mainly a weaponless system of fighting (offense) or self-defense. It can be divided geographically into **Northern style** – North China, Peking=Beijing - more barren, more use of legs, walking huge distances, vast distances between centres, people generally larger in size. Cold, historically home of the capital cities, scholars and royalty - *Northern Mantis, Xing Yi Quan, Tai Ji Quan, Eagle Claw, Chang Quan*, - showy performance Wu Shu forms, *Ba Gua Zhang*, technological developments. Come from the north.

Southern style – South China, Canton=Guangzhou - fertile, agricultural/warm weather, entrepreneurial, people generally smaller size. Strikes, arms, fists more hand techniques, *Wing Chun, Pak Mei* (white eyebrow), *Choy Lay Fut, Hung Kuen.* Crane style, 5 Ancestors, *Nan Quan, Jow Ga.*

Today's Chinese Kung fu mixes it all up. North / South / internal / external

Peking or as it known today, Beijing, was and is the capital in the north, not only the cultural centre, but also the centre of education, technology and finance. This continues to today. There exuded a sort of snobbery that northerners looked down on their southern cousins. Unless or until a "something" was validated in the capital, it was probably considered more of a "folk art" or even a worthless pursuit.

Furthermore, styles are classified as:

Nei Gong/Ni gong – internal/ seems to have been explored more by northerners. *Tai Ji Quan – yin yang boxing, Yi Quan – mind boxing, Xing Yi Quan, BaGua Quan- 8 trigram boxing.*

Hey Gong/Wei Gong - external styles/*Hung Kuen, 7 animals, strength based hard musculature Karate.*

Chinese kung fu migrated to Korea, where we have *Tae Kwon Do, Tang Soo Do and Hapkido* and east to Okinawa and Japan where there developed a myriad of styles – *Karate* (empty hand- in fact used to be called China hand) *Judo, Aikido, Jiu-Jutsu, Sword Kenpo*. Through my small time with Aikido in Adelaide, I learnt the foundation of the sword in empty hands, it seems the most skilled strikers come from understanding the sword or *Bokken* (wooden staff/sword). These days, most accomplished Martial Artists agree that all styles have a mix of internal/external, you could even say everything.

The **Chi** [vital life energy] should be excited, The **Shen** [spirit of vitality] should be internally gathered. The postures should be without defect

QI GONG aka CHI KUNG

My initial encounter with *Qi Gong* was in Yangshuo, Guangxi Province S.W. China. Participating in Papa Gao's *Bu di Zhen Qi Gong*. It hit the marker for me, a strong vehicle for me to sign up with the school... Even though I had roughly 20 years of Chinese kung fu behind me, I had never tried *Chi Kung/Qi Gong* before or really understood what it was, so I decided to follow Papa and his Bu di Zhen school to get more deeply involved.

A typical Qi Gong session began with the 12 moves, there would be pools of sweat on the floor upon conclusion, I felt it was really cleaning me out and I adored it. Then It became fully internalised for me, I later found out we do a type of "Iron Shirt Qi Gong", we would then proceed to Tai Chi which I found difficult to internalise (maybe lazy, maybe stupid). As Papa spoke no English and Bu di Zhen is a folk martial art, the Gao family were not particularly scholarly, I was never exposed to the philosophy behind it, I guess possibly mistakenly I craved an intellectual engagement; that came later as I purchased books in the Shanghai Foreign languages bookstore and bought copious amounts of videos. Later with Lily Sifu of Chen Xiao Wang Chen Tai Chi in HK- we did Ba duan Jin - 8 pieces Brocade Qi Gong (which I had learnt from video in addition to Yi Jin Jing. I love all of them, but as Zhang Sifu told me *"Tai Chi is Qi Gong"* after showing me some ball expansion exercises. The Mainland Chinese government seems to have classified most of China's kung fu into Wu Shu paradigms and Chi Kung is no exception.

The 3 main qi gong mainland exercises being:

1. Ba Duan Jin (8 pieces brocade),

2. Yi Jin Jing (Muscle/Tendon Change Classic)

3. Wu Jin Jing (5 animals frolic).

The lesser-known sets of Bu di Zhen and Master Se are falling into obscurity. It's a privilege to be aware of these sets. There was a very good website tackling a lot of China's lost arts and forgotten masters. Unfortunately I can't remember it except the dude was acting out of Shanghai.

FB Guangzhou 2005

...After the fiery Lucy disappeared on me in SZ, I took a muso job playing in a new jazz club in Guangzhou on Ersha Dao (Ersha Island), near the art gallery. Contractually, it was supposed to offer a room each. In SZ with Zhang Shifu, we loaded up the smallest van with all my stuff and chugged along the highway from SZ to GZ. Upon arrival in GZ, I was put in a flat with the band-leader, *uncool* ! After accepting a months wage in advance, and working for a week I did a runner, calling Zhang and the van back, we did everything in reverse back to SZ...

qi gong cont.

These days I prefer a more gentle method of Chi Kung, although I must say the internalised papa's short breaths has returned since I had a heart attack, it feels like I can draw in pure oxygen through my nose. It has been said that exercising muscles and limbs generates and accumulates Qi.[1] Papa Grandmaster Gao reminded me of a shaman when Mum unfortunately caught pneumonia in Yangshuo while staying with me. Papa would come over to give a Qi Gong session in her recovery. He started by hovering his hand over parts of her body then began singing/reciting what sounded like a shamanistic sound.

Shamanism is a practice that involves a practitioner reaching altered states of consciousness in order to perceive and interact with a spirit world and channel these transcendental energies into this world. All *exercise* is GOOD!

From my understanding, Huangdi Emperor - *Yellow Emperor* - created dance-like movements in conjunction with breath to the benefit of himself and his people to overcome sickness through stagnation. Over the years the influence of Buddhist ways - such as meditation/ breathing/ yogic traditions/mind use, along with the development and marriage of Taoism – Daoism (a Chinese manifestation) with folk ways and the Buddhist ways all contributed to the existence of Qi Gong. *Qi* = air and *Gong* = skill – Air Skill. Including Kung Fu.

Master Jwang Ming believes that Qi is bio-electric energy in the body as Qi hasn't been scientifically proven to exist. I believe Dr. Yang, Jwing Ming and add that I believe it is connected neurologically along and through the nerve pathways and that the Jingluo (meridians) are primarily nerve pathways that have electric current. Neurons are electrically charged. It is claimed by some masters that Chi Kung is Tai Chi Chuan and vice versa.

What is **internal** ? In my journey, it began as a magical mysterious energy called "*Chi*" that resides in the chi areas of our bodies internally - *lower abdomen/dantian*. Flowing through meridians throughout the body. Science has not proven "Chi" or meridians (in mando - Jing Luo). Master and doctor Yang Jwing Ming likes to call Qi- Chi *electric current* or *bio-electricity*. Chi =Qi not scientifically proven is to the Chinese an energy that resides in specific areas of de body and flows through meridians which are like pathways, similar to veins & arteries of which blood flows. Qi flows through meridians(jingluo) Meridians are called Jing Luo in mando. I believe as neurons are electrically charged & are stored in the brain by the shitload. The brain being neuro related sends the electric signals along nerve pathways synapses etc. The body is full of these nerve pathways, which in my opinion could be the meridians. Proving Dr Yang correct in stating qi = bioelectricity.

Jing ze = Spoof, it is to my mind *life essence,* and for me, the *Jing Luo Qi* meridians are lined up along our nerve pathways. Do nerve pathways transport electric current? Yes, neurons are electrically charged and are found by the truckload in our brains - Neuro = nerves. This could then mean the nerve pathways are meridians & qi is a recognised neural energy along with our natural God given energy? Electricity is energy neuro is bio electric this could match to qi and meridians being nerve pathways???

chinese k fu cont'

In ancient days, military incorporated use of weapons- spears, swords, projectiles to name some, to achieve the upper hand in battles. Weapons also joined the Kung Fu curricula.

Recently a Tai Chi master's defeat by a mixed martial arts (MMA) fighter last week has renewed debate over whether traditional Chinese martial arts is practical in real combat.

The Tai Chi master, Wei Lei, took a pounding at the hands of MMA fighter Xu Xiaodong when they faced off publicly in Chengdu, Sichuan province last Thursday. The duel was over in 10 seconds, as the video footage posted online showed. Wei's defeat, which internet users have described as "humiliating", shone the spotlight on the practicalities of Chinese martial arts – is it useful in combat or just a form of exercise? Again a fighter, knocked out Tai Chi dude Ma Baoguo in less than 30 secs recently – "Kung fu fakery"? And how did it evolve through the centuries into what it is today?

The reality is fitness, a kung fu man who does core exercise, jogs miles a week - his core being strong - as is his cardio respiratory systems (Bruce Lee? Then how'd he die!?), an elderly tai chi master who has mainly done slow space walking, no gym work/core/cardio etc. obviously doesn't stand a chance GA LA WOR!

China's martial arts history goes back more than 2,000 years, and has contributed to the country's culture and even literature (wuxia – kung fu novels), with Chinese novels often depicting heroes' superior fighting skills. But Chinese martial arts, also known as kung fu, have been practised for millennia for a wider range of reasons than just combat.

We can look back at its history through the dynasties. Monks practiced kung fu at the Shaolin Temple in Dengfeng, Henan province.

Hired killers and Gladiators

The history of Chinese martial arts goes all the way back to before the Qin dynasty (221-207BC) began. In the hundreds of years prior to the Qin dynasty, many dukes and noblemen hired professional killers to safeguard their interests or invade their enemies' territories. Later, like in Rome, some wealthy families bred gladiators, forcing them to fight for their spectators' entertainment.

When Qin Shi Huang (Yellow Emperor) unified China under his dictatorship, his government suppressed those professional killers and the military aspects of the skill. But their combat tactics were passed on, albeit more as a form of art, taking on elements that resembled dance, drama and acrobatics.

Beggars and Street entertainers

In the 750 years between the Tang (618-907) and Yuan (1279-1368) dynasties, commercial martial arts organisations sprouted across China as the commercial economy developed in Chinese cities and towns. Many martial arts practitioners took to the streets to busk for money, showing off their skills or challenging their audience to duels.

Soldiers, Mafia and the CCP

During that time, especially in the Song dynasty (960-1279), some governments boosted the teaching of martial arts in the face of regular threats from invaders. Skilled soldiers and generals who could fight well were particularly valued. A variety of weapons were invented or improved for battle during this period.

But as China progressed into the Yuan and Qing (1644-1911) dynasties, new governments ruled by ethnic minorities began banning the use of weapons in martial arts practice. A form of Chinese boxing gained popularity instead, which was later used by Qing rebels to build up mafia organisations across the country. (boxer rebellion). After the People's Republic of China was founded in 1949, people started taking up martial arts as a form of exercise and the CCP promoted Chinese Martial Arts as a nationally accredited sport.

FB China 2013

...Again I am the guitarist in aussie sax ace Blaine Whittaker's band, we are backing Michael Man Dat Wong, and meet at the HK post office near the Star Ferry, to hop in the latest gizmo people mover to drive to Foshan, Guangdong China for a 2 day gig. Absolutely incredible how China modernised itself in such a short time - ain't no fucking mucking around there. However the Chinese government is proving itself to be a big bully, and we wouldn't know what hardship and frustration the local people/peasants would have gone through for the president to get his way to modernise.

It's easy to marvel at such "progress' but what went down?

We fly along super highways to *Foshan*, historically the centre and birthplace to a good number of Chinese Kung Fu legends, namely *Ip Man*, *Wong Fei Hung* and *Bruce Lee* family!

Arriving at *Foshan*, I see a mostly flattened area with a lot of construction and shells of buildings soon to be majestic high-rise. A common sight in China. In the distance there seems to be a completed high-rise, and that is our hotel, the InterContinental. Porters rush out to greet us and after check-in we're told to meet back down in the foyer, I wander around, totes aware of kung fu, see little statues of Bruce Lee with his nunchakus placed in salient points in & around the foyer. I am buzzed, so that arvo I take a circular walk around the man-made lake adjacent to the hotel. Hoping to find a reticent kung fu master, nothing reveals itself so I engage in a bit of *Wing Chun* and Tai Chi by the lakeside and realise I have walked about 10k's to complete the circuit.

Next day I wander to the nearby ultra modern shopping plaza to find a coffee, only to witness quite a few white western babes there on their phones. Funny place China!...

WATCH: *Wu Gongyi versus Chen Kefu in Macau, 1954*

https://www.youtube.com/watch?v=2FsZyPjsjTA

:):):)

k fu history cont'

Sportsmen, valuing performance over prowess. During the early twentieth century as the Qing dynasty was being overthrown, Chinese martial arts gained a new status – as a modern sport. In 1936, China's martial arts team performed at the Berlin Olympics. Kung Fu becomes sportified.

A brief update on Chinese Kung Fu legends

Yue Fai (b.1103)- *eagle claw Xingyi master martial artist/war man*

Huo Yuanjia (b.1868) - northern kung fu legend part of the *Shanghai Guo Yu Jing Wu* kung fu school, He is portrayed by Jet-Li in the movie *Fearless*, and avenged by Blee in *Fist of Fury*.

Wong Fei Hung (b.1847) - Hung Kuen expert Son of legendary *Wong Ka Fei* -Foshan/ South China stylist - portrayed in the movie series *"Once Upon a Time in China"*.

Ip Man (b.1893 ~ d.1972) - *Fo Shan Wing Chun* exponent who introduced Wing Chun to the world via HK and Bruce Lee. Ip Man movie series starring Donnie Yen.

Sun Tzu (544 BC) -military strategist/ author of *"The Art of War"* probz the book guide for ccp.

Fong Sai Yuk – Fictional Guangdong dude linked to the Southern Shaolin temple(never confirmed).

Bruce Lee (b.1940 ~ d.1973) – US born, HK bred, part Western blood American Chinese innovator of Chinese martial arts and movies. Jeet Kune Do kung fu style(way of intercepting fist) a first MMA.

Passed away from Heat stroke leading to a brain complication, possibly a Hemorrhagic stroke (probably glad he didn't survive). Five movies that changed the world - *The Big Boss, Fist of Fury, Way of the Dragon, Enter the Dragon, Game of Death*(not completed).

Dong Hai Chuan (b.1797) - Creator of Ba Gua Zhang boxing

Chen Fake (b.1887) - leading Chen man exponent of explosive Xin Jia/teacher/.

MasterChen Xiao Wang (b.1945) - current living hero of Chen style Tai Ji Quan, one of the 4 living masters.

Yang Lu Chan (b.1799) - student of Chen style, later taught what would become "Yang Shi style Tai Ji" beginning in Peking, later with his sons exporting it to North America and the world. Tai Chi - O - movie.

Zhang San Feng - 12th century inventor of *tai chi chuan*.

Australian Kung Fu legends: Guy Le Claire, Earle Montaigue, Serge Ermoll, Joe Bugner. Richard Norton, William Cheung.

Shaolin -Buddhist temple in mid Henan province North China/ beginning point for Indian martial arts to morph into Chinese martial arts. The name refers to the woods of *Shaoshi* (少室; Shǎo Shì) mountain, one of the seven peaks of the Song mountains. The first Shaolin Monastery Abbot was *Batuo* (also called *Fotuo* or *Buddhabhadra*), a Dhyāna master who came to ancient China from ancient India or from Central Asia in about 464 AD to spread Buddhist teachings.

Wudang

A small mountain range in northwestern Hubei province renowned for the practice of Tai Chi and Taoism as the Taoist counterpart to the Shaolin Monastery, which is affiliated with Chinese Chán Buddhism. The Wudang Mountains are one of the "Four Sacred Mountains of Taoism" in China and an important destination for Taoist pilgrimages.

What is Magic?

It is defined as:

1. Paranormal (beyond the scope of normal scientific understanding)

2. Illusion (a deceptive appearance or impression) Many ancient cultures have used the rituals of magic, not- withstanding the Chinese.

Magic may have aligned with kung fu and propagated. The teachings of Pang Sifu encourage us to know how to manipulate our body weight and body mechanics focusing on our waist, being aware of our weight COG (centre of gravity). Pang Sifu used to say Bruce Lee knew about this stuff. As said to me also by T.S.Tsang (author of many kung fu books).

MAYA India /Central America?

Māyā meant *"wisdom and extraordinary power"* in an earlier older language, but from the Vedic period onwards, the word came to mean *"illusion, unreality, deception, fraud, trick, sorcery, witchcraft and magic"*. However, P. D. Shastri states that the Monier Williams' list is a "loose definition, misleading generalisation", and not accurate in interpreting ancient Vedic and medieval era Sanskrit texts; instead, he suggests a more accurate meaning of māyā is "appearance, not mere illusion"…….Aliens at work.

What is Qi Gong?

According to my Zhang Shifu, *Tai Ji is* **Qi Gong. Author** Ellae Ellinwood states "one must understand qi – the force of life & the storehouse of vitality. Every culture has a name for the energy that animates all life - qi,chi, bio-energy, prana, spirit. Qigong has a rare ability to include everyone in its experience & to adapt to the needs of different groups without losing its own character in the process. Self-healing disciplines, **spiritual renewal groups,** marital arts, medicine, Buddhism, & Taoisim have all incorporated aspects of qi gong & benefitted from its gifts." It is naturally entwined in China's cultural history.

The four Chinese internal martial arts comprise - *Tai Ji, Xing Yi, Ba Gua* and *Liu He Ba Fa*. And ***all*** are considered Qi Gong. To be honest, I am still learning in this field.

I have not mastered the essence of qi gong, I have learnt moves and concepts, but I am not Master.

Parahansa Yogananda states that life force enters into the body through the Qi or chi. This *chi* can mean "air" = *Hei* in canto. Hei gung - gong returns as "skill"- air skill - like Gong Fu - Kung Fu. Back in Shaolin Temple, Henan Province China, the ole Indian monk Boddhidharma (possibly a *kalaripayattu* Alien) arrives to find the Chinese monks wasting away from lack of exercise so he teaches them some moves, It lasts and morphs into…? Good ole *Shaolin Kung Fu!*

The Yellow Emperor - Huangdi (600BC) embraces the Qi Gong classics *Yi Jin Jing (Muscle/Tendon change classic), Wu Xing Jin (5 animals frolic), Ba*

Duan Jin (eight silken movements) and this becomes China's staple exercise diet, later embellished by imagination and magic. Yellow Emperor's classic of medicine.

According to Master Gary Khors book "Tai Chi"... Huang Di holed up on the banks of the Yellow River, only to witness that with floods, the stagnant water left in the fields and villages left a putrid stench, disease and death to living things. Observing this he understood that human aliens need to never be stagnant and he created sets of dances (qi gong sets) for the people to exercise. Besides studying with Pang Sifu, I followed Yim Sifu's *Tai Chi Gong* (wushujia.org) for about 6 months, we meet every Wednesday and Tuesday, (eventually for me it boiled down to just Wednesdays with the larger class in Shaukeiwan).

Yim Sifu's huo li TAI CHI GONG 2015

I began this practice that I enjoyed in Shaukeiwan with Esther and the gang. Introduces 8 exercises in static position that introduce the participant to the fundamentals of Tai Chi. Along with health preserving characteristics, It often reminded me of a religious gathering, as the hall was full of raised hands in the air. In class we do postures standing and sitting in chairs. I wouldn't call it a deep qi gong experience, more like a social gathering to participate in a sporty tai ji qi gong routine.

Sifu Yim Yee Chung, fifth generation Wu Style Taijiquan descendant, disciple of fourth generation Beijing Chapter, Wu Style Taijiquan Grandmaster, Master Li Bingci. Graduated from the martial arts school of Fujian University of Education, he is now the Chief Executive Officer of 'Wushujia', choreographer of the Huoli Taijigong, Chairman of both 'Wushujia Foundation' and 'Huoli Taijigong Association', and President of the 'Wu Style Taiji Association of Hong Kong, China'.

Yim Sifu is from Fujian Province, China and has been involved in Kung Fu his whole life. His passion in martial arts began in high school. He went to the University of Education and devoted himself in studying various martial arts, including the external vigorous *Waijiaquan* and the internal soft *Neijiaquan*. He also studied human body anatomy and cure on sports injuries. He graduated in sports science at Uni, and partook in the ceremony of *"Baishi"*, Master accepting student in 1999. *Bai shi* year also means seniority.

An interview I conducted with Yim Sifu:

1. Yim Sifu, can you please give me a bit of background about your history in Kung Fu. How you got started and where? 嚴師傅,請問您可否簡介一下您習武的歷史,您是何時在何地開始您的功夫的?

嚴義松老師,**吳**式太極拳第五代傳人,師承北京**吳**式太極拳第四代掌門人李秉慈大師;福建師範大學體育教育學士,主修武術;《武術家》總監、活力太極功創編人、《武術家慈善基金》主席、《中國香港**吳**式太極拳總會》會長、《活力太極功總會》主席。 嚴老師來自福建,初接觸武術始於中學階段,也因爲熱愛武術也喜歡教學,因此報考福建師範大學體育系,其間**涉獵了眾多體育種類**,包括屬於外家拳的武術,與**內**家拳的太極拳與八卦掌;也修讀了人體結構及運動創傷治療等相關課題。 以下是嚴老師個人事業的關鍵年紀:

• 1994年末,嚴老師在北京外語學院進修,常到紫竹公園學習**吳**式太極拳,後經霍

Yim Sifu

• •

•

2008年,與首批學員與太極拳愛好者在香港成立《中國香港**吳**式太極拳總會》,冀能更專注發展**吳**式太極拳。

2010年末至2013年初,獲李嘉誠基金會的「香港仁愛香港」集思公益計劃撥款,實踐了三個回合的【活力社區】項目。第一回合的項目,更獲選為最佳項目實踐獎之一。'活力太極功'就是在這個機遇下誕生。

2012年《武術家慈善基金》,2015年《活力太極功總會》也相繼誕生,不同組織不同組合,但殊途同歸,為的也是推廣健康,傳承國粹。

Here below are the major turning points of Sifu Yim's career in chronological order:

..

...

In late 1994, Sifu Yim met Master Li Bingci in Beijing. The charismatic Master Li taught Wu Style Taijiquan with clarity. Sifu Yim's interest grew day by day and he gradually devoted to it.

In 1995, Sifu immigrated to Hong Kong, and worked at a special school run by Caritas. He studied and practiced taijiquan when he had time, kept in touch with his teacher and mentor Master Li, and shared what he knew with fellow taijiquan fans.

In 2004, with the support and encouragement of his family, Sifu Yim quit his full time job, and integrated his career and mission into one. 'Wushujia', which means all martial arts practitioners belong to one family, was established.

In 2008, Sifu Yim and his first batch of students established the 'Wu Style Taiji Association of Hong Kong, China', to foster the study of Wu Style Taijiquan and concentrate on its development in the community.

From 2010 to the beginning of 2013, Sifu Yim successfully obtained grants thrice from 'Love Ideas Love Hong Kong' of "Li Ka Shing Foundation'. It was under these circumstances that 'Huoli Taijigong' was choreographed. The first round project was granted one of the best performed projects. This is one of the reasons why this set of taijigong is named 'Huoli'. The three projects sponsored by 'Love Ideas Love Hong Kong' are 'Huo Li She Qu', which literally means 'Vibrant Community'.

1998, Sifu Yim formally became the disciple of Master Li by a *'Bai Shi'* ceremony. It is both a recognition and respect to his teacher, and a pledge to spread taijiquan as his mission from Sifu Yim to his teacher Master Li and the Wu Style ascendants.

'Wushujia Foundation' and 'Huoli Taijigong Association' were born in 2012 and 2015 respectively. Different entities with a different mix of people, yet they carry the same mission of fostering the tradition of martial arts and for promoting the betterment and health of the community.

2. Currently, I believe you focus mainly on Wu Tai Ji and Tai Ji Gong? 2、以我的理解,您現在主要集中於練吳太極和太極功,對嗎? 是的。 現在教學上,大概70-80%時間用在吳式太極拳及劍,餘下 20-30%的教學內容,有八卦掌、武術(包括:長拳、刀、槍、劍、 棍、槍、南拳等)、推手對練。免費推廣的,主力是活力太極功,輔以養生棍增加趣味性。

Yes. Around 70 to 80% of his teaching time is for teaching Wu style taijiquan and sword, with the remaining 20 to 30% on baguazhang and various martial arts including long fist, broad sword, spear, stick, nanquan (quan of southern style), and push hands.

For promoting health consciousness, Sifu Yim teaches Huoli Taijiquan for free. He also adds health preservation style stick training to make the training more interesting and avoid boredom.

以下是為何選取吳式太極拳的原因:

Reasons why he chooses Wu style instead of other forms of taijiquan:

The characteristic of 'Wu style taijiquan' can be summarized in sixteen words: Qing, Jing, Rou, Hua, Jin, Cou, Shu, Shen, Chuan, Zi, Bu, Xing, Xie, Zhong, Yu, Zheng'. These 16-word principles help us to understand what is 'exercise our body externally while retaining vitality and strength internally', and 'use our mind but not the force'. As our mind leads our movement, the body should be in a relaxed mode (as versus a stiff and tense state). The 16-words also help us to understand using key joints of human body, like shoulders, elbows, wrist, crotch and knees, and the lever principle for every movement of taijiquan. Unlike other styles, Wu style does not have heavy stomping nor jumping, and hence is more appropriate for health preservation & elders.

Longevity and health are key elements for leading a meaningful life. As many Wu style taijiquan masters live long, it is considered that the practice of Wu style taijiquan contributed to this to a great extent.

3. Can you please tell me how and why the Tai Ji Gong exercises came about? Did you invent them? What are the benefits of such a workout?

Also where do you see the future of Tai Chi Qong gaining international recognition?

Taijigong could be a static posture, or a series of movement aimed at gaining internal strength. Every movement of the taijiquan could be a static 'taijigong' posture. Through repetitive practice, one can gain internal strength and energy. 'Quan' and 'gong' are inter-related. Just practicing 'quan' and neglecting the 'gong' will end up nowhere in taijiquan pursuit. Only through practice and with solid hard work on the basic 'gong' could one transcend the quan practice to a higher level.

Huoli Taijigong

Introduction: Huoli Taijigong, choreographed by Sifu Yim, is a series of concise, simple, absorbing the essence of taijiquan movements, suitable to do either standing or sitting. Huoli Taijigong targets the community at large, like office workers who are in a sedentary position most of the time, eyes concentrated too much on the screen and hand too much on the mouse, unconsciously bending forward either in front of a computer screen or a cell phone screen. Sifu Yim also aims at preventing illness as critical illness as various forms of deterioration seem to hit us at younger ages.

Future Development:

Sifu Yim, of course wishes 'Huoli Taijigong' to gain international recognition. From early 2013 until now, we have been promoting 'Huoli Tajigong' on our own without any sponsorship. We seize opportunities to showcase the public and provide courses with a minimal administrative fee. If opportunities knock in the future, we will assess our manpower and resources and see what we could do. To spread health consciousness to our community has a long way to go. We sincerely invite the following persons to sponsor or work with us:

1. Organisations: Working with you to promote 'Huoli Taijigong' to another sector of the community.

2. Funding: With funding, we could train more coaches, and they in turn could organise more courses in their neighbourhood and spread to different areas of our community wide and fast.

3. Community Leaders: Please support us with whatever forms of sponsorship, be it your expertise, resources or connections.

4. I hope you don't mind but I am doing the exercises with some students here in Australia. it seems a lot of people think of tai ji as a healthy exercise, a flow of movements, more like a dance. the quan aspect is omitted. Perhaps a lot of foreigners aren't aware that it is actually tai ji quan... any thoughts on this? But the Aussies I have met here, seem to have a good grasp and understanding of qi gong. Both tai ji and qi gong are separated by the western mind. What do you think of qigong? Is there a separation of such in Chinese thinking? To me tai chi is a kung fu, without the quan/kuen then it seems to be a type of qi gong? I know Ba Duan Jin and Yi Jing Jin, they remind me of healthy exercises without pugilistic involvement?

4、我希望**您別介意**,現在在澳洲有一些學生跟我練太極。在很多人看來,太極是一項由很多動作組成的健身運動,有點類似舞蹈。但是'拳(武、好鬥因素)'的部分

Taijiquan is a form of Chinese martial arts. Together with *Xingyiquan* and *Baguazhang*, they are known as *Neijiaquan* 'internal martial art'. Taijiquan originates from the health preservation quan aspects of Taoism. It derives from the attack and defense principle, and develops the technique into philosophical wisdom of 'winning the strong with the weak', 'defeating swiftness with slowness', and 'conquering majority with minority', and 'retreat in order to advance'. Taiji is commonly used to mean Taijiquan. Taiji culture is rich. It includes taijiquan, taijigong, taiji weapons and taiji sparring. Taijiquan is Chinese martial art, widely known as wushu or kung fu. However, without the combat 'quan' element, they are not necessarily Qigong. Baduanjin and Yijinjing do not have the 'quan' element. However, for their health preservation value, they belong to the health preservation Qigong, which is different from the 'hard' fighting qigong. Though Qigong and Taijigong are different in style, they share many things in common. Yim Sifu Huo Li Tai Chi Gong with Esther Sihing

Thanks very much for your time Yim Sifu and Esther Sihing. Best Wishes Always - Guy xxx

I remember our 8 moves

1. I call *pushing the heaven up to sky*

2. I call *wings flapping and flying*

3. *Two hands in defence and throw - both sides*

4. *Guiding the ball from both sides using the waist*

5. *Inverted side arise hands push down in front*

6. *Step out push* - perhaps *Tui Sho*

7. *Engage the mind*

8. *Stand on tippie toes then sinking and*

sliding the torso to the knees.

Most of my students like this routine.

There is a quiet certainty that I will recover with Yim Sifu's way, even though he doesn't speak English, Esther is there to guide me. We move onto exercises with a pole/stick, these ones kill me as I think my shoulder is frozen.

T'AI CHI CH'UAN CHING Attributed to Chang San-feng (est. 1279 -1386) as researched by Lee N. Scheele

In motion the whole body should be light and agile, with all parts of the body linked as if threaded together. The **Chi** *[vital life energy]* should be excited, The **Shen** *[spirit of vi- tality]* should be internally gathered. The postures should be without defect, without hollows or projections from the proper alignment. In motion, the Form should be continuous, without stops and starts. The **chin** *[intrinsic strength]* should be rooted in the feet, generated from the legs, controlled by the waist and manifested through the fingers. The feet, legs, and waist should act together as an integrated whole, so that while advancing or withdrawing one can grasp the opportunity of favorable timing and advantageous position. If correct timing and position are not achieved, the body will become disordered and will not move as an integrated whole; the correction for this defect must be sought in the legs and waist.

The principle of adjusting the legs and waist applies for moving in all directions; upward or downward, advancing or withdrawing, left or right. All movements are motivated by *I [mind-intention]*, not external form.

If there is up, there is down; when advancing, have regard for withdrawing; when striking left, pay attention to the right. If the *I* wants to move upward, it must simultaneously have intent downward.

Alternating the force of pulling and pushing severs an opponent's root so that he can be defeated quickly and certainly. Insubstantial and substantial should be clearly differentiated. At any place where there is insubstantiality, there must be substantial- ity; Every place has both insubstantiality and substantiality.

The whole body should be threaded together through every joint without the slightest break. **Chang Ch'uan** *[Long Boxing]* is like a great river rolling on unceasingly. *Peng, Lu, Chi, An, Ts'ai, Lieh, Chou,* and *K'ao* are equated to the Eight Trigrams. The first four are the cardinal directions;

Ch'ien/Nan [South; Heaven], **K'un/Bei** [North; Earth], **K'an/Guang** [West; Water], and **Li/Xi** [East; Fire].

The second four are the four corners: **Sun** [Southwest; Wind], **Chen** [Northeast; Thunder], **Tui** [Southeast; Lake], and

Ken [Northwest; Mountain]. Advance *(Chin)*, Withdraw *(T'ui)*, Look Left *(Tso Ku)*, Look Right *(Yu Pan)*, and Central Equilibrium *(Chung Ting)* These are equated to the five elements: **Earth, Water, Fire, Metal** and **Wood**.

BUDDHISM

Buddhism and its philosophies are never far from a real kung fu man, historically speaking the creation of Chinese kung fu began in a Buddhist Temple -*SHAOLIN* in central east China. In popular culture, the 70's "Kung Fu" television series featuring David Carradine, espoused the subject, bordering on a fusion of Taoist philosophy. I believe the two: buddhism & taoism merged and lived intertwined creating a somewhat mysterious culture for the average *Joe Blow* to understand. It has taken me decades to even have an inkling of understanding on this topic. The *sinicized* fusion of Buddhism and Taoism with the addition of animism and folk religion.

Reeling from a shift in the Australian Music scene in 1989, now living in St. Peters adjacent to Marrickville, and too much rock'n'roll lifestyle, along with a Dad who had been changed overnight into an incapable man by a stroke, and one brand new baby boy, I was spinning out of control with frequent dilapidating panic/anxiety attacks, I couldn't even drive down Marrickville Rd. to the doctors without freaking out and pulling over to the side of the road. Each doctor at the Medical Centre had different opinions on my pathway forward, one advised imbibing prescription drugs (which actually made it worse), one advised a different lifestyle/ exercise and diet (which I later embraced), further on down from the medical centre on the same road was Dad in a horrible depressing Marrickville 1980's nursing home. I knew I couldn't leave him there for the rest of his days, along with my deteriorating mental state I ran up to the Blue Mountains to stay with Mum at her cute place in Katoomba. The first night I took some meds to calm me down but this felt totes wrong. I knew deep down inside, the Doctors suggestion of a lifestyle change was the way to go. It is incredible how we can find our own positive pathways within ourselves. Mum kept suggesting I go to the Australian Buddhist Vihara for meditation. I had tried a few different mind yogas and TCM with panicky results, so I left those ones alone.

Now based at Mum's in Katoomba. I took the Katoomba-Sydney train one day and ended up sitting opposite Venerable Tapodhana from the Australian Buddhist Vihara for the two hour trip. We smiled and got talking. I was aware he was a monk by his robes and instinctively thought small talk may not be the go. However by the time we arrived at Central two hours later, all was good. I began attending the Australian Buddhist Vihara's devotion/meditation sessions (Vipassana) Therevada Buddhism. Bhante, the head Monk and Rene the administrator became my friends and guided me along in my practice, finally I reached a calm, with the attacks subsiding, therefore I became more interested and devoted, completing several retreats over the next few years, learning the Pali Liturgy.

'Namo Tassa, Bhagavato, Arahato Samma Sam Buddhasa, Budhan Saranaan Gachami, Dhamman Saranaan Gachami, Sanghan Saranaan Gachami'.

By 1991, Dad eventually moved into the big house Sylvia and I bought in Katoomba a few streets across from Mum. Everyone had their own room, I was having a family! Earlier in Sydney, my good friend Carl Orr had organised a few meetings and chanting at the Sydney Nichiren Buddhist Centre in Arncliffe, I attended these and the germ of Nam Myo Ho Renge Kyo was planted (1987). I was quite fascinated by my Theravada Buddhist studies in the Blue Mountains, I did sense the order /clergy (Sangha) seniority over the layman vibe, and helped build the Stupa with gusto. By 1994, the family had *split up* with the wife and kids moving to HK. During 1995 with me missing my kids who were thousands of miles away, I hopped on a plane to visit them. Upon leaving to go back home again to Oz and with my son bawling like mad at the airport, it affected me very much. I felt I couldn't go on with my current life, studying at UNSW for a Music Masters Degree, working at AIM (Aust. Institute of Music) and participating in a relationship I was unable to fulfill.

So in a semester break I moved into the Buddhist temple. After a few weeks it dawned on me that I have to take charge of my life and get back to my kids. So I ran upstairs and told Bhante head monk that I'll be leaving, and I did.

The Vietnamese Airliner heading for Saigon then Hong Kong, flew right over Katoomba with Dad in the Burlington Nursing Home and Mum below. It was a ducking hard decision, but it gave me another 7 years with my kids.

As I settled into a fake and imaginary money obsessed HK lifestyle, my spiritual devotions got swept under the carpet.

Naturally I did have aspirations, I would once a year go to Yangshuo in SW China to "get back in touch". It wasn't until I was living with Li-Yin post stroke at I-Uni Q in ShaukeiWan that I ran into a musical colleague- John Mallig, who encouraged me no end to attend some Nam Myo Ho Renge Kyo chanting sessions at Kaikan. He was adamant it would help me, I am in about Nov 2014, so I went enthusiastically. First the Causeway Bay Kaikan, met

Derek, John was amazed I lasted the time of the Gongyo and Daimoko without distraction or leaving (a cuppla hours). He is very encouraging and inspirational. Eventually I attended the big meeting at the HK Soka Gakkai headquarters (a very impressive piece of HK real estate) in September 2014 I would run from ShenZhen where I was kung fu training to receive my HK Soka Gakkai member certificate. As time went along my faith and dedication to this Japanese Mahayana Buddhism grew in strength and I still practice today. **Nam Myo Ho Renge Kyo** the essence of the Lotus Sutra.

2nd October 2016

I proudly received my Gohonzon in Adelaide as a stroker from the Aussie Soka Gakkai leader Chris Steins. I still chant, though perhaps not as vigorously as before but it is certainly embedded in my system. Bell used to think of it as baloney and annoyingly I've had to rescue my Gohonzon a few times.

Remember ~ We **all** have **KUNG FU**.

Be it

Farmers, Farming, Car/Truck Drivers, Mechanics, Tradesmen, Musicians, Doctors, Nurses, Allied Health Professions, Artists, Engineers, Public Servants, Inventors, Swimmers, Footballers, Cricketers, Surfing, The Gym, Carers, Caregivers, Hospitality, Teaching, Transport Workers, Dancers, Ballet, Painting, Painters, Skiing, Skiers, Cycling, Chefs, Cooking, Climbing, Scientists, Writers, Ambos, Emergency Volunteers, Firemen, Paramedics, Australian Defence Force, Police etc ~

Thankyou Heroes!

My take on it is Exercise **EXERCISE YOUR BRAIN, EXERCISE YOUR BODY**

What it boils down to is a **KUNG FU** is a lifestyle and attitude, all encompassing, all embracing, A Passion, Addictive, Unending.

We get into it, We are it and it is Us!

Do Everything You Can To Overcome ~ Please Don't Hurt Any Living Thing ~ Be Aware.

Chant *Nam Myo Ho Renge Kyo*

THINK OF THE NOBLE EIGHTFOLD PATH

Within the Fourth Noble Truth is found the guide to the end of suffering: the Noble Eightfold Path. The eight parts of the path to liberation are grouped into three essential elements of Buddhist practice—moral conduct, mental discipline, and wisdom. The Buddha taught the Eightfold Path in virtually all his discourses, and his directions are as clear and practical to his followers today as they were when he first gave them.

THE NOBLE EIGHTFOLD PATH

✦ 1. Right Understanding (*Samma ditthi*)

✦ 2. Right Thought (*Samma sankappa*)

✦ 3. Right Speech (*Samma vaca*)

✦ 4. Right Action (*Samma kammanta*)

✦ 5. Right Livelihood (*Samma ajiva*)

✦ 6. Right Effort (*Samma vayama*)

✦ 7. Right Mindfulness (*Samma sati*)

✦ 8. Right Concentration (*Samma samadhi*)

Diet and food for thought...

One of the most important things we have to consider is diet. What you put in your body Hippocrates said,

"Let food be thy medicine, Everything in excess is opposed to Nature"

You are what you eat..

May I now recommend to you to try some Kung Fu, Tai Chi, Chi Kung, Walking, Meditation, Breathing exercise for both physical & mental improvement. Start slowly & softly. Disengage for a while...

HK December 2015 Post stroke *Li Yin...*

It's time for me to leave Hong Kong as I'm flat broke, can't work and there is no sustainable social security net I will not have LY support me indefinitely, thats not fair and I no money la!. It's a rough time and decision to leave, both hk & Li Yin who has really taken care of me during and since being out of hospital. I am forever grateful, and hope I can repay her one day. As well as terminating my near 30 years of calling Hong Kong *"home"*. I am very upset and feel heart broken as I had always hoped to return to Oz successfully. I will be returning a 'disabled' on ya gooouuuyyy!

On the 12th, we have a little trip to Hainan Island... I am totes sad ...the future is uncertain...

Up above the South China Sea heading for Haikou on Hainan Airlines an American drawl welcomes us aboard, all is good until the taxi that we get stops 800 metres short of the hotel and the driver kicks us out, luggage and all, I'm fuming "Can't he see I'm disabled?!!" Only the strong!

The hotel turns out to be really lovely, right on the coast with views to the mainland across the strait, its facilities are fabulous. Li Yin has booked a really good deal, I'm so lucky I can walk, by now, 36 months later, we set off to explore, first along the beach then into Haikou town, we walked heaps and all day, I was looking forwards to my Taikoo Shing fave *"hai nan chicken"*, we find a sort of kitchen hall/court/mess, and it's not available, WTF!!. Anyway food was good and interesting, we uber home (uber convenient in China), 4 days go by sweetly with the dreaded last day on our minds. This is when I would truly be alone for the first time, I was worried.

On the last day we get to the airport, check me in back to HK, Li Yin has to get a bus down to the airport train station to get on a train to central south Hainan to visit her grand parents. Once outside and getting her on the bus then watching it disappear, nearly kills me, I howl! I Fucking hate airports as they are always tied in with separations and shit. I am mighty upset, this incredible woman who nursed me to recovery so I could take a trip like this has left. Tears falling on the ride back to HK. I stay the night in Li Yin's place at Lohas Park (lifestyle of health and sustainability - a massive residential complex comprising of towers that rise 45 stories high, each floor with 5-8 flats, a totally unreal place) I get up early the next morning thanks to Li Yin's flatmate Ean, hop in a taxi to the airport and I'm on my way to Australia on Singapore Airlines.

Arriving in Adelaide the next morning to warnings of a *Super Heat Wave*, I exit out the arrival hall to see Mum and my son Julien. I won't see Li Yin for another four months till we meet in Sydney.

May I say to my readers, at this stage of the book closing off the Chinese kung fu section, before moving onto more memoirs. That taking up a kung fu in your recovery is a very positive thing to do. It can be any kung fu something learnt & achieved over time, it could be your existing kung fu skill or just joining a Tai Chi/ Qi Gong class. As I notice some deterioration with my body, I become more determined to get out and do it. Using both my yi gong and awareness of muscles, joints & balance, working on these I believe will contribute to my quality of life.

Memories

CHINA 2003 – pre stroke

Arriving and settling in China was just like a Clint Eastwood spaghetti western. It was a fucken' trip (2003). I had a ball living in China for 3 years. Moving to the village of Yangshuo in South West China and living a full-time Kung fu life was extraordinary especially in such a beautiful location.
https://www.istockphoto.com/photos/yangshuo-county

However, right now I am back in my country –Oz – 20 years later and the opera China is playing is NOT cool! A revisit to Sun Tzu's Art of War may give an idea of what the scoundrels are upto.

'Know when to fight and when not to fight: avoid what is strong and strike at what is weak. Know how to deceive the enemy: appear weak when you are strong, and strong when you are weak. Know your strengths and weaknesses: if you know the enemy and know yourself, you need not fear the result of a hundred battles.

The Art of War summary

This is my book summary of The Art of War by Sun Tzu. My notes(James Clear) are informal and often contain quotes from the book as well as my own thoughts. This summary also includes key lessons and important passages from the book. In fact most of it applies to kung fu warriors...

- "According as circumstances are favorable, one should modify one's plans."

- "All warfare is based on deception. Hence when able to attack we must seem unable. When using our forces we must seem inactive. When we are near we make the enemy believe we are far away. When far away we must make the enemy believe we are near."

- "Appear weak when you are strong, and strong when you are weak."

- "If he is superior in strength, evade him."

- "Attack him where he is unprepared. Appear where you are not expected."

- "The general who loses a battle makes but few calculations beforehand."

- "There is no instance of a country having benefitted from prolonged warfare."

- "A wise general makes a point of foraging on the enemy. One cartload of the enemy's provisions is equivalent to twenty of one's own."

- "Supreme excellence consists in breaking the enemy's resistance without fighting."

- "The worst strategy of all is to besiege walled cities."

- "There are five essentials for victory: He will win who knows when to fight and when not to fight. He will win who knows how to handle both superior and inferior forces. He will win who's army is animated by the same spirit throughout all it's ranks. He will win who, prepared himself, waits to take the enemy unprepared. He will win who has military capacity and is not interfered with by the sovereign."

- "If you know the enemy and know yourself, you need not fear the result of a hundred battles. If you know yourself, but not the enemy, for every victory gained you will also suffer a defeat. If you know neither the enemy nor yourself, you will succumb in every battle."

- "One may know how to conquer without being able to do it."

- "In war, the victorious strategist only seeks battle after the victory has been won."

- "In battle, there are not more than two methods of attack: the direct and indirect."

- "An army may march great distances without distress if it marches through country where the enemy is not."

- "You can be sure in succeeding in your attacks if you only attack places which are undefended."

- "Military tactics are like water. For water, in its natural course, runs away from high places and hastens downwards. So, in war, the way is to avoid what is strong and strike at what is weak."

- "Let your plans be dark and impenetrable as night, and when you move fall like a thunderbolt."

- "Ponder and deliberate before you make a move."

- "A clever general, therefore, avoids an army when its spirit is keen, but attacks it when it is sluggish and inclined to return."

- "It is a military axiom not to advance uphill against the enemy nor to oppose him when he comes downhill."

- "The art of war teaches us to rely not on the likelihood of the enemy not coming, but on our readiness to receive him."

- "Make your way by unexpected routes and attack unguarded spots."

- "If they will face death, there is nothing they will not achieve."

- "The principle on which to manage an army is to set up one standard of courage which all must reach."

- "If it is to your advantage, make a forward move. If not, stay where you are."

The Art of War by Sun Tzu overview by James Clear

I know how they think..it's about revenge against the world /for historically the world pillaged and raped China, now with an outdated traditional mindset they are wanting payback – a long scheme - the world had better prepare for. Additionally most middle to upper class mainlanders think foreigners that live & wk in china are there because they couldn't 'make it's back home. There is a big underlying dislike on the racist front.

The pacific islanders are proving stupid to my mind bringing in China. There will never be an immigration policy inviting them to china. Unlike oz that welcomes them openly as they carve careers in sport, care & trade work here. Hey China ... just let Taiwan be u bullies.

Also no regard for conservation/climate as they seek with money to buy up KOLOMBANGARA Solomon Islands for its forest, deep water port & strategic. Dumb fucks over there will be fucked! The islands will end up looking like the environmental negligence of its major cities, Guangzhou, Beijing, etc.

CHINA shot down mh 370.

To note with my reader the history of the British method into China was a disgusting one. As they ran out of a payment currency to pay for tea, which became a British past-time cuppa tea? Existing to today ja? The scoundrels began a low brow exchange of opium from their British India. Which was accepted by the doped out tai chi masters? This acceptable trade commodity spread, naturally throughout the land, hooking the population on it! Much like the crap today of big pharma!

back to my marvellous china experience for 3 years pre stroke of course

I adored living in China - the sights, smells ingrained a joy in me plus the people were lovely. Living there I was in a constant buzz state of being.

Yangshuo YS village, Guangxi Province South West China 2003

Firstly, I must say I was located in a strong ethnic peoples occupied area. The Zhuang people being the majority of the first nation people of Yangshuo, their approach to life may have been the joy I had here. Generally speaking Han Chinese the majority of China's population are steeped in hard work & money money money no laughter is heard generally, ethnic people chilllaugh more. Training in the Budizhen Yangshuo kung fu gym (located in picturesque Yangshuo) was *de riguer* daily. Using weights, striking techniques, punching bag forms. It was right up my alley. I was living in a kung fu wonderland. I loved living in China, I was there for a total of three years. In Yangshuo for a total of near 2 years, OMG how I loved this place! Felt like I could live out my last days here, a juxtaposition of the most simple Chinese peasant life with the advancing China of tomorrow it was terribly exciting! I always felt safe and I admired Hu Jin Tao, the then president. Often I would bellow *"wo ai zhung guo"* (I love China) when I was pissed. After a time I would bellow *"wo ai zhong guo he ao da li ya"* (I love China and Australia!). The youth of China have so much more respect, grace and awareness than the HK youth and most young anywhere. China is novel I am taken in with its simplicity, culture and cheap prices along with being in the country of Chinese kung fu. I engage big time. It was also quite cheap in those days...accom, food, transport. Simple living & kung fu training.

Yangshuo along with the towns Dali and Lijiang embed themselves in your mind if you are an avid reader of *Lonely Planet*. All three I've been to, they are located in Southwest China. Guangxi, Guizhou and Yunnan provinces. SW China represents a stunning locale, inhabited by colourful ethnic people and super-duper geography, new sights, culture and smells. A strong sense of unfamiliar and adventure.

An aspect about these provinces was that a high number of ethnic people live there the Miao, Zhuang, Dong, they all had their customs, cuisine, fashion, arts, craft and music. It was a refreshing ascent from the unsmiling Han Honkers. I absolutely adored living there, Cycling- wise, YS was perfect, flat with easy tracks circumnavigating the majestic lime stone peaks, like *"moon hill"* etc. Yangshuo – a stunningly beautiful area in Guangxi, lies downstream the picturesque Li river from Guilin City. I was a bike kung fu master in YS along with Scott (BikeAsia).

With the appreciative help of Budizhen Master George Gao, I managed to secure a 3 bedroom flat for 800 kuai a month (about 100 aud), right next to the Budizhen school and the theatre that showcased the ethnic performance troupe nightly right on Xi Jie (West St). At least once a month I would go back to HK to gig and bring rent money back. George taught me the prices of things and where the best noodles etc were. Being naive re these things in China, especially tourist spots like this one, resulted in one being continually ripped off. You needed to have your wits about you.

I got myself into a routine I enjoyed very much. Up early by HK standards, into the Budizhen kung fu gym with Papa Gao and his twin sons George and Peter. Immediately engrossed into some folk style of Qi Gong. Finishing with a pile of sweat on the floor. And Chi energy moving from hand to hand.

Hopping on my HK bought Specialized bike, I would trek around the overwhelmingly beautiful countryside, or settle into my music zone in my well setup flat.

The ole George and Peter liked smoking and drinking beer, like most males in China. So with continual encouragement to smoke, we did. Then it was lunchtime, which meant a trip to the shop down the Lane on *xi Jie*. West Street to imbibe the cheap local *Liquan* beer. I must admit it was a bit of a paradox to be training so hard, then consuming. After all this I would retire to my very cool flat and work on my music.

Most of the younger Chinese people of which there were many residing in YS, initially hope to gain English language skills as YS was known across China as *the natural English corner of China*. For example: Each park in a Chinese city has an area, usually in the corner of the city park, with a sign posted saying *"English corner Wednesdays 7pm"*. Everyone who wants to learn or practise English will meet there at that designated time. So, Yangshuo is the natural English corner of the nation because of it's natural beauty, scenery, location & abundant English schools.

This *English* corner of China has dozens of English language schools that hire foreigners to teach. It equates to employment & a rather easy pursuit of a date or language exchange sessions, which I pursued to gain a grasp of the Mandarin Chinese language and Mainland Chinese Culture. This proved to be fruitious. I self studied with these new friends having no Mandarin I eventually established a fundamental ability to speak their language. I began to understand so much more, and the mainland logic was satisfying, compared to Hong Kong – I had spent the previous 7 years in HK unable to grasp a logical thing except for money.

I learnt the Pinyin Mandarin system, which then enabled me to pronounce any Chinese word fairly accurately, unlike the HK Canto system which is a joke... for example: Tsim Sha Tsui, a vibrant Kowloon district with a Bruce Lee sculpture on it's Avenue of the Stars is actually pronounced more like *jim sa joy* and Mongkok is *wonggock*, Shatin - *saa tin*. Go figure. All that used to do my head in, it was like the Cantonese purposely creating a mindfuck preventing gwai-loz (foreigners) from pronouncing the language correctly. And with a debilitating hearing defect probably the onus was on me not hearing accurately as the initials in Chinese are unlike English and then there are tones, one wrong tone renders the word another meaning. I had to use memory graphic systems.

Finally here in China was a good method to learning Mando and I got it! Also geographically speaking, it was simple and logical. Learn **bei = north: nan= south:xi** = west: **dong** = east: and voila you had all the provinces sorted ... ie. *guang dong province* (guang to the east- right), *guang xi* (where I lived *guang of the west* or left!), *Shan dong*, *Shanxi*, *He nan* (he in the south/down - home of tai chi) *Hebei* (he of the north/up) *Hunan*, *Hubei* etc. etc. Good stuff! Logical yet most Hong Kongers don't get it. The Li River is famous for its stunning scenery of Limestone Karst peaks, and lush countryside. I first went to Yangshuo with my family in about 1994, I would return each year solo to the *Balcony Hotel* for a week to deal with life in HK, cycling, chilling, beer drinking and writing music was the routine. Getting back in touch/ Nature God etc.

So it was no surprise that I took the kids there in 2003 to get away from SARS in HK and a stubborn wife who would not move back to our condo in Melbourne, Australia. Within the first few days and after settling into the Balcony Hotel, we happened upon Twins George and Peter Gao of the **Budizhen International Kung Fu School**. The twins were muscle-lee and displayed impressive kung fu moves so I enrolled the three of us: myself, daughter Stassy and son Julien. We started training immediately. Grandmaster Papa Gao - George & Peter's Dad - introduced me to Qigong, a new venture in my life and one I became occupied & intrigued with. By the end of the 12 moves in one position qi gong, I would be sweating like a pig, I felt better, like I was getting all the crap out of my body and gaining new skills, this I decided was gonna be my path (like the popo -Yuen Qiu -in the

Wudang TV series in HK she leaves her family for a pilgrimmage to Wudang). After sitting the kids down and telling them my plan, I took them back to HK and school and arrived back in Yangshuo solo, later in life there would be immense repercussions on this decision, with both my kids ignoring me (I lived back in the Blue Mountains for 10 years with only a couple of visits from my son and daughter).

George helped me immensely in creating a life in YS. Found a flat near our school just off Xi Jie St. This place, Yangshuo, was a tourist spot & incredibly beautiful, so it did have a strong party element, booze was cheap with plenty of bars. I didn't mention to anyone that I was a professional muso. I just quietly slipped back to HK once or twice a month to gig, get some gig money, my rent was cheap. The locals saw me carting guitars to the bus stop and always asked about it, so slowly they guessed I was some sort of muso, I took that overnight "Yangshuo to Shenzhen" bus so many times. Luckily it had beds, on arrival 12 hours later in Shenzhen at the border of hk & china, I would go for coffee and ham 'n' eggs in my fave restaurant. HK freaked me out, and I would be so happy getting back home to Yangshuo. I trained hard and began developing muscle tone. The training in *Tai Chi* I couldn't adhere to because it was just numbers (each move was a number, I later found it easier to remember a move by its name or concept) and no understandable philosophy – deep conversation excluded me due to my language inability. I think my mind was expanding somewhat, intelligently and intellectually since I was living alone.

My basic instinct could not memorise the forms taught in numbers, our school only had Lao Y- (foreigners). But the ole Qi Gong I loved and can remember it all to this day. I later discover that we were doing a sort of martial *chi kung, hard style, iron shirt qi gong* (Legend Yue Fei's teacher Zhou Tong was a master of various "hard qi gong" exercises.), involving little bursts of inhalation through the nose with tongue on roof of mouth. Every physical exertion since I did would involve this breath thing into the gut. Now I don't do it so much as I don't believe it to be so healthy, more natural slow rhythmic breathing is better, I think. I still remember the 12 moves, very physical short bursts of breath into the lower abdomen – dantian in coordination with a move. In static position, feet shoulder width apart and straight/parallel, clenching fists we would begin, onto a sort of blocking move, bending down and scooping - like gathering energy from the earth and a double hand hit on your gut and push out then one hand like a bell or a beak behind the *ming mun* (back door) opposite *dantian*, and the other like a birds mouth / beak up in the air brought down to the ground - like eating and flicked up both left and right sides in frontal side stance, next was double hands or what I call kangaroo paws blocks, all moves involving strong short inhalations of breath finishing up with qi gong self massage and Qi awareness. I found it invigorating and fascinating as a pool of sweat lay around me on the floor. The origin of Budhizhen lies with Papa originating in Shan dong (mountain east:), a fusing of shaolin and wudang practices. The moves didn't have names just numbers. I remember it.

Yangshuo was a repository of many expat foreign nationalities, who then created their own little communities. We had the British - mainly English teachers who were popular with the kids and school bosses, hard working, frequenting the pubs, then the Aussies, based around Bar 98 and Climbing Bars, the French, based around the Balcony Bar et Le Votre run by twins Luc and Christophe Vincent, ex French Armed Special Forces soldiers and Budizhen alumni. Tour operators are also based here, hanging until their next group arrived.

As a free spirit I seemed to exist in *all* the communities, drifting and befriending at will with the players. It was quite amazing really as I seemed to be accepted by them. However whenever I tried to speak French it came out as a gurgled mix of French and Mando. Night times were so much fun in YS.

https://www.youtube.com/watch?v=vcEkgKpP_bk

The Climbing Bar, up near the end of Xi Jie was run by a hip bloke, so I confided in him that I play guitar. He arranged for a performance, which was taken well "but do you sing!?" I got booked to perform weekly. One arvo while setting up, a loud raucous American from Shanghai was at the bar, I decided to go over and see what was happening. In his loud drunken voice he declared *"Chinese women FUCK with your mind!!!"* Later I discovered this with Gina and Lucy.

So I began playing twice a week at the Bluebird Cafe for dinner, with the French violinist across the street, after I would run up to the Climbing

Bar play a couple of sets after dinner, then run all the way down West St. with all my gear on a big trolley to Bar 98 run by Snow and Scott for a late set.

I had bought a sort of Bose copy PA in Guilin. Chinese cities have areas specifically for certain goods and there is much to choose from and usually cheap. I made a daily routine of AM kung fu training / cross country cycling (absolutely glorious in these neck of the woods) and then PM practicing, singing, learning songs and composing in my very cool flat. Gerry, my Kiwi mate gave me a copy of Jeff Buckley's GRACE album, well that turned my head around. I wished to sing. After about a month of running around on the weekends, other cafe owners would run out of their establishments saying as I dashed from one to another *"you come play my place!!!"*.

It was quite funny and I guess it elevated my status to join the other YS existing cast of characters like William (the Chinese *Picasso* who sold his wares on the Xi Jie (west) street), Malcolm (Vietnamese/ Aussie with the best restaurant on the corner), Josh (mad American that wrote and sung *"Stayed in YS Way Too Long"* now settled back in Michigan with his Chinese sweetheart). To me, Josh & I were like Harry Nilsson & John Lennon existing in a mad haze of over consumption talented tho', except we weren't in the Bahamas, we in China, Duck (the German english teacher, whose students all spoke english with a German accent), Joe the Turk, Alf (yangers.com creator), Snow and Scott (owners of Bar 98 and BikeAsia), George(Rip) and Peter (always getting around with no shirt on/muscles with a rogue look and attitude, funny fuckers) and the Banana lady.

There was no live music in the village then in 2003, now every bar and cafe has it.

Budizhen Kung Fu YS:

The actual Budizhen School was really a dingee old building/ gym. It was totes like in a movie you'd expect Stallone to appear in moments notice:). Finally I was living in my dream kung fu movie and in China!

In hindsight I think the focus on hard breath and Fa Jin, may be too much for beginners. One will find that most Chinese martial arts or systems are shrouded in mystery as the art has been mostly passed on orally. However I now believe with time & research you can find a **linkage** through all styles – kung fu. Keep it simple.

This Gao family kung fu style Budizhen, a small family/folk martial art steeped in both Shaolin & Wudang moves & principles. Papa Gao(RIP) sits as Grandmaster with his twin sons George(RIP) and Peter Gao as the lineage holders(George used to call me 'wanking master':). I am a 4th disciple holder and a number of Papas former descendants and disciples are in Australia and Europe. It is reputed that Papa came from Shandong up north and played Sun Wu Kong with opera troupes, he certainly had an entertaining manner displaying impressive *Pole/Sabre* manoeuvres whenever someone new came to school. Through my years as a Hong Konger, I could see his moves on the opera stage. We had about 3 Qi Gong forms that I focused on and learnt. We had and about 3 Tai Ji Quan forms which were recited in numbers i.e. *move 1/2/3/20/55/ 80/102*etc. I couldn't memorise them. It wasn't until I learnt Chen Tai Ji with the names of moves ie: *lan zha yi /jing gang dao dui/ dan bian,* that I could remember. The tranliteration name of move worked better with my intellect than a number. Say dan bian I can … say no 89 I can't.

Anyway, Papas *Tai Ji* always looked like a kung fu form to me, confusing me in my western belief of what Tai Ji is. Probably most westerners think tai chi is always a slow moving, peaceful slow set of movements non harmful etc. thats what I used to think … but it is called tai ji quan it is a martial art! I still can't do the form, I can visualise moves, probably render a fakee set for yaz. thankfully the *budizhen sets* and related are preserved in France by Masters Hrod and Sabine Romero of *Wandering Dao/Dragon Tigre Ecole.*Southern France.

https://www.youtube.com/watch?v=4X742UgmXGI

Apparently the Budizhen style is an amalgamation of Shaolin and Wu Dang kung fu. I would imagine this to be common all those years ago as Chinese Daoist concepts blended with Indian Buddhist ways. I was awarded 4th disciple status in 2004.

FB George & Jack, a budizhen alumni - have requested all students of school be present in a minibus taking all of us westerners of the school to

Liuzhou city, for an event of opening a new building project headed by the local bigwig. We are all supposed to be from various consulates – upon arrival we are told all booze and food plus happy endings in the sauna house are on the house.

As you've seen, I had a ball in Yangshuo and at the school for a year and a bit. We used to do weights/ bag training, stretches but no sparring really, there were fights & often our students got into fights and won. Strangely we didn't have any Chinese students, all Lao Y(foreigners). There was a bit of huffing and puffing, along with posing off with musclee bodies & ego at times also. After a stint as school administrator, and getting with Lucy Long Feng (fiery Miao girl). I began to find the politics of our school and the village became a nuisance and a bit overwhelming. Lucy left for SZ so I decided to follow her and lived in Shenzhen for a couple of years. So it was goodbye YS for a while(I went back later with Alex for a few months).

I developed an enlarged thyroid, which I put down to a lack of selenium in local Chinese produce. I am not a doctor, so I operate on instinct, and I developed heart arrhythmia later, leading to AF Atrial Fibrillation. Papa Gao it was said was sick of his heart playing up so he thumped it whilst down by the picturesque Li River where training had begun to take place(kicked out of the gym by comercialisation), and it killed him. He did live to be in his mid 90's and was teaching me and others right throughout his 80's he was an inspirational master and character. I became the 4th Disciple of the school in 2004.

FB: Yangshuo 2003 ...The American guy in the Climbing Bar is screaming at me exclaiming *"Chinese women fuck with your mind!"*. My first girlfriend in YS was Gina, her story began in Ningbo and discovering that her husband was cheating on her, she would pop pills and end up in some Ningbo disco totes out of it. Eventually some business man from Guilin invited her to stay with him to help her get over this self destructing behaviour. She accepted and ended up in YS to learn English, & I ended up in bed with her indulging. A pattern evolved whereby she would constantly say she was staying with girlfriends in Guilin(an hour down the road), during her *period* ended phase. Later I found out she was still seeing the Business man (sugar daddy?). Next was Echo, one very intelligent Uni student from Shi Jia Zhuang, who ended up fucking the young boss of The

Climbing Bar, she lost the plot after he treated it like a one night stand, we chatted heaps and probably rooted with our minds until she left. YS had a lot of transits. I then got the complete hots for Lucy, a half Han/ Miao girl.

https://www.youtube.com/watch?v=uEMXHix_thE

Shenzhen SZ 2004-2005

I lived in Shenzhen for 2 years, at first in Dong Hu a district with lovely Lucy (a half Miao spunk), I have my red Specialised bike with me so each day I ride to Donghu Gongyuan (Donghu Park), looking for a Tai Chi teacher, after having studied full time BuDiZhen Tai Chi in Yangshuo for a year which is not classified or recognised as a nationally sport accredited style, I am determined to find a recognised style (Yang, Chen, Sun & Wu styles are recognised). Upon entering the park under the friendship bridge one is confronted by many so called "Masters" displaying signs and paraphernalia about their wares, I carefully examined them daily and settled with Mr. Zhang Guang Wen Shifu in the far end of the park. Zhang shifu hails from Zhengzhou, capital of Henan Province (birthplace of Tai Chi) his teacher Gou Kong Jie is a well respected Chen style Grandmaster "If you want to watch *Chen Style Tai Chi* performance, see Chen Zheng Lei. If you want to know who is the best practitioner see Chen Xiao Wang. If you want to learn *Chen style Tai Chi* follow Gou Kongjie" said Master Liming Yue.

I immediately began in earnest cycling every day to the park by 9am, regardless of lack of sleep from a gig in HK & the commute the night before. Zhang began with basics, stance work, moving. Chan Si Gong (silk reeling) Ski squats all this for about 6 months before we moved onto the form of Lao Jia (old frame).

Once on the form I was captured by learning each move has a name, rather than a number like in Budizhen, ie: *"Buddha's Warrior Attendant Pounds Mortar (Jin Gang dao Dui)*

- Six Sealing and Four Closing (Liu Feng Si Bi)

- Turn Left and Buddha's Warrior Attendant Pounds Mortar (Zuo Zhuan Shen Dao Dui)

- Buddha's Warrior Attendant Pounds Mortar (Jin Gang Dao Dui)

Dan Bian, these are so ingrained in me I can't forget them, upon exiting the stroke hospital I couldn't remember most of the form, now 3 years later it is coming back. I trained everyday -Tian Tian- *Chan Si Gong/silk reeling* is a most important practice, so we did it all the time. I came to appreciate its subtlety and meditative aspect. Chen Zheng Lei has said "people with all sorts of ailments have come to his workshops in Chen Jia Gou (birthplace village of *chen tai ji quan* in Henan province) and left healed like a miracle after playing Chan Si Gong!" Zhang and I became best of friends, he has a son but had split from his wife, they were still up north. He charged his students by form, and lived simply in a grotty unit provided rent free by his student in the same estate as me, I lived with him for a time there, when Lucy's chilli temper freaked me out.

I witnessed my own improvement and progression, I saw the logic in it all, I was way into it. I felt so positive & happy that I found this Kung Fu, I was making it 'My Kung Fu'. You can too!

Lucy split, I moved into a sort of long term hotel next to Shenzhen gymnasium, I was still trekking most days to HK for gigs, I had a spare bedroom, so Zhang stayed with me, as my Mando was basic meaning deeper more involved tight discussion would evade me, I hired Xiao Zhang (little John) from an advert as translator, given his fees were affordable at the time and we also developed a good friendship. Zhang Shifu and I trained hard taking photos at the modern futuristic Gym grounds. It was here that Zhang encouraged me to compete in the 2006 International Wu Shu Competition HK "BiZai".

Upon hearing my name as a winner in the comp at KITEC, I was ecstatic! What a Blast! Mate Rickard & Maree Malmsten were there, I collected my gold medal and certificate and hopped on a Kowloon bus headed to Hung Hom station to get train back to Shenzhen, called Mum and Shifu on de buss in excitement. Since then, I have moved so much I lost that darn gold medal & video footage, darn it. I must have been the fittest I would be as I trekked/walked all over SZ or cycled, lugging guitars to & from HK for gigs, training everyday with Zhang.

https://youtu.be/g8gHqh4oH9Q

with Zhang Shifu in the park SZ

https://www.youtube.com/watch?v=otCH33iUrTM

with Zhang Shifu in the park SZ

I remember dragging Lucy to the shenzhen bookstore in a parkee area near a park where kites were flown & buying copious amounts of books on chinese kung fu. For me it was glorious the mainlanders flock to bookstores reading in the ailes. Luv dat!

FB...Trekking every second day across the border *Luo Hu Koan* to do gigs was really doing my head in, the mainland still treated foreign HK Permanent Resident holders as "Foreigners" we couldn't access the HKers line which moved quickly, so I had to trudge along with occidentals, backpackers, business people in the foreigners line taking forever

, it was so funny once a bizman with a wig/rug gave his passport to the immigration officer and this officer kept looking at the man then his passport looking totes perplexed wigged out. Wednesday nights I was with Swedish talent & entrepreneur gifted bassist Rickard Malmsten and brother Robbin Harris at the *Bohemian Lounge* and the following night at *Geckos* with Robbin & Linus run by Christophe. I was trekking back & forward a lot!

Guangzhou GZ

I first visited Guangzhou in about 1997, when HK was getting to be too much. Along with Macau in those days both Macau & GZ were HK escape hatches, GZ easy to get to, just hop on a direct train (old style – old days) from Hung Hom Station, Kowloon up to the border via Sheung Shui, then marvel at the fact that one is now in China just under an hour. From GZ station I headed straight to Shamian Island, a lovely area full of old colonial buildings and leafy parks opposite Qingping street market and straddling the Pearl River. I quickly checked into a backpackers, unloaded and went for a long walk. In the process of this walk I found quite an old colonial style dilapidated city, in which most of the old buildings lining the street were built over the footpathways, creating a heavy shadowy darkness, at this moment I wished I hadn't booked a few nights and could just go back to HK. Having paid the accommodation already I persevered and eventually found it quite fascinating. Qingping market certainly was an eye opener, all manner of animals for sale- dogs, cats, snakes, things id never seen. As the years went by I frequently gigged in GZ, nearly every weekend in fact with **RED**. I came to like GZ as an alternative to HK, pretty wild place!

Shanghai

After a sojourn for a resident gig in Guangzhou, I then return to SZ but with no Lucy to be found. Not long following a conversation with my mate Shanghai based drummer, Nicholas McBride, and a suggestion by him "come up here, you'll find work and it's good and get over Lucy" I decided to take the punt. Shanghai had a lively live music scene with some really cool jazz clubs & musicians. Again I packed my stuff into boxes, Zhang Shifu helped me get it to the train station to send it up to Shanghai. I later fly up, coming into land at Hongqiao Airport where I could see a thick smog in the atmosphere. I had been to SH before with Sylvia. We were based around the "French Concession" Huai Hai Zhong Lu where I kept running into a Frenchman from a wealthy family in the Huai Hai Starbucks. He was studying Sanshou, and reckoned he picked up chicks in this Starbucks for some bonking around the corner in his crib.

On this sojourn I stayed in a box of a room in a motel and called Barbara, my mate Mark's beau. She picked me up and took me to all these little nook and cranny local style restaurants. Blabbering in Shanghainese and drinking lots of beer, we had fun. I then moved into the Shanghai Conservatory of Music dorm on Fenyang Lu, French Concession. My hope to become immersed in the SH pro music scene flopped and my old school mate Dikran B. bailed me out. I can't remember exactly what happened.

I must have gone back to SZ and gigs across the border, until I holed up with Alcoholic Alex in his nice pad in Futian SZ, right near the *Futian Kouan* (HK border) my mando was still pretty shit, I had achieved a beginners communication exchange level from my days in YS, a lot of resident foreigners actually spoke quite well, and the locals got used to it. The locals were mainly innocently curious, very hospitable & respectful "Ni hao chi fan mei you?" - a polite 'hello' translated literally to – 'how are you have you eaten?' They would feed you if not. I did encounter some lawless moments, but on the whole I dug being in China. The people displayed emotion, respect & passion. The Arts and Music touched their souls deeply. I never used Kung fu, people in the parks would come over and offer their advice in tai ji qi gong activity. Loved the parks!

My final time in SZ was training with Zhang Shifu, commuting to HK for gigs non stop & living with booze addled Alex, who by now was not paying the rent, so eventually we did a runner from that place, I took him to YS, where we both got English teaching jobs with accommodation. I lasted about 3 months in YS, while Alex shackled up with a bird, staying on. Life gets a bit blurry here, but I believe I went back to HK, and it was here that his girlfriend called me from SZ to say Alex died in his sleep. Without a passport, ID or visa, the authorities would not release his body for a funeral. So I had to go over and confirm his id and body by going to the morgue, a ghastly horrible experience.

BEIJING:

I have gigged in Beijing quite a few times, the 1st time I arrived you could say I was in a state of both fear & overwhelmation. Coming in from the massive airport into a downtown area on a freeway it looked to me like another world. Mark's mate Jeff showed us around over the next few days, the hutongs were being pulled down SADLY for massive concrete dumps to be erected. Tiannamen square freaked me out, it's vastness & history overwhelmed.

China is incredible.

HONG KONG

Hong Kong an incredible juxtaposition & creation of potent Chinese & Western existences. Clearly the British engineers created a marvel, no doubt the locals where gobsmacked and sent their kids OS to gain such magical skills... Hong Kong strikes you like a real kung fu stroke / chop with it's engineering marvel, sounds, smells, density - an aural & visual feast Big Time, the locals contributed big time also by hard work & business acumen. Bellisa had reservations about HK as an Indo, however when I took her there thanks to Samantha & Olaf Vogee my ex boss, she left loving it!

I love Hong Kong deep. Clearly Hong Kong is one of the most unique & amazing cities in the world! I gave HK the best most productive years of my life. Nothing regretted, thank God I'm an Aussie.

A dream I had with brother Robbin Harris....

.....We had been in HK So long but we were both leaving, somehow we were going by ship or huge ferry to the airport, boat pulled out from Central to go to your stop Kennedy Town, I could see you running down the road to the pier, once you got on you wouldn't sit with me at the stern. You sat up the front. You were gonna be the first to fly, back to Canuckland, as we pulled out into the harbour, I overcame my stubbornness and joined you up the front to be with you in the magnificence of the harbour vista, we were picking off all the places we had played. In the overwhelming emotions, we knew we weren't coming back. We bawled our eyes out.... I woke up.

"always strange creative people gather in the centre of money" Ryuichi Sakamoto

To be clear, I had two periods of living in Hong Kong...

I Love Hong Kong. A lot of people ask me about the handover in 1997.

I was stationed in the high class Conrad hotel the night of the ceremonial handover , perched above the convention centre where the handover ceremony took place, my band hired for the event, in a lavish room filled to the tilt with buffet an incredible amount of food etc., for the whole time duration we never saw any guests. They de bosses had hired another room in the Marriott with a better view to the occasion, the lavishness & excess of HK at times was sickening, me my band were not allowed to partake in any of the over the top buffett, and no one came!

Some locals wandered around with PRC flags mostly derros, Finally as a stroker the 2015 umbrella protest movement crippled HK, forcing mtr train stations & all transport to a halt, it was a bit scary however I was just an expat dude. Kung fu master. The CCP moved in altering the basic law which leaves a sour taste in my mate & expats, we don't want to go back.

HK for me was the most amazing time & eventually to call HK home was an honour. The first period was from 1979 to 1981 (I was in my early

20's tourist visa). I lived on Lamma Island, Yung Shue Wan, and began Wing Chun studies, as well as having secured my first professional gig.

The second period was from 1996 to 2015 (I was in my 40's pr visa, married to a HK girl), in which I secured PR status citizenship with a three year hiatus living & studying tai ji in China during this period, the latter part of this HK time period as single, I was based in the beautiful area of Sai Kung and Clearwater Bay(2006-15), having spent the initial part in high rise lacklustre Shatin with family(1996-2003). Also in this 2nd time period I managed to carve out a successful professional career as a musician.

HK One 1979-1981

I first arrived in HK with Mum in November 1979 after leaving my job at Berny's Radio, Mosman and flying off from oz with Mum via a jaunt around Indonesia and Thailand. Mum's dress design business was going really well and she had two places in Yung Shue Wan, Lamma Island. One where she lived and 2nd a flat/studio right in the villagethat I rented off her. We are, along with the Derricks and Dale Wilson, the original western Lamma-ites. I took over mums 2nd place at 55 Back St. Yung Shue Wan. This place/village reminded me of a Mediterranean style fishing village a la Chinese, lapping bay waters with a beer or snack or seafood at hand facing Yung Shue bay & an incredible city just 20 mins away by ferry that could rival NYC. I fucking loved it! Stayed until, immigration kicked me out. Mum had right to abode but I didn't, that came later in 1996, and then in 2003 I obtained PR status, which really is like citizenship. It was here in Lamma at the first stage that I knew I would become a professional musician and a kung fu guy. Kung fu and Guitar were my constant 'go to'. Totally dedicated & impassioned.

I had studied guitar and music for a couple years in Bondi with Peter Andrews at the Academy of Guitar, so I knew what I had to work on and got to it, practising all the time & self educating. Met the likeable, fluent Canto speaker and gifted musician pianist American Dale Wilson (now music professor at Columbia University). We immediately formed a band with Ajax and Ricky. I witnessed my own progression as I practiced hard and found Sifu Po Kin Wah / Wing Chun. It was an idyllic life having the hideaway of Lamma Island and a big super exciting yet Alien city like Hong Kong.

After a time I met Sylvia who in some ways was just a village girl from Sham Shui Po (a district of many in HK). We hit it off, even though she initially liked Dale (American fluent canto speaker that looked like Jesus), we started dating, and I found the Chinese femaleness, intellect & vibe, cute and refreshing. We entered a loving relationship sharing no doubt bruises as we both came from broken families, my desire to protect and make happy evolved. I dug Sylvia & her funny little family - Sim Tse(amah), sisters Connie & Florence, Dad - Gung Gung and learnt a lot about HK and her culture.

My time was up, no more visas and an entre to Berklee College of Music meant in 1981 I took off for Boston USA. After time there, I was with Dad who was now living in Paris. My mind was continually on HK and Sylvia. *Duality.*

I told Dad I'd go back to Australia via HK. But knew I'd stay in HK, as I did. I can't remember this phase right now, but eventually without HK PR I got kicked out, landed back in Sydney in time for the Conservatorium of Music summer jazz workshop and a jazz studies- audition with Don Burrows and George Golla. Nervous I was, they failed me and my dream was broken! Basically with a patient father, I slogged my way along on guitar studying/practicing finally reaching national touring with famous bands in the 1980's earning a reasonably good wage(more on this in my My Kung Fu Music book). Sponsoring Sylvia to Oz, where we married, had two kids, bought a house in Sydney's inner west then Katoomba, Blue Mountains. Mum was also living there.

I took on a job after touring for more than 10 years as head of the guitar department at the Australian Institute of Music (AIM) in 1991 and with five days a week commute from Blue Mountains to Central, Sylvia and I started to drift apart. Finally I split, she couldn't cope so well, so on her mother's demands went up to HK with both the kids, and has stayed there ever since.

One day in 1996, while I was living in the Australian Buddhist Vihara on Cliff Drive Katoomba, with the kids in HK, I went to Bhante the head monk and said "I'm going to HK next week, my wife hasn't concluded on divorce and I can't be without my kids". He said "good", and I left.

Here began my second period of living in HK.

HK Two 1996-2015

In 1996 with the loss of the Keating Government, I decided to leave Australia & head OS to HK. My kids and legal wife (we agreed to no divorce) were based in HK. I headed for HK to see if things could be patched up & be with my kids. In hindsight, the forcibly separation of leaving my family (dad & mum) & country, then developed a mental Illness of hate, resentment abcdefghijklmnopqrstuvwxyz phobias, where I was hell bent at fucking up my wife for such an unplanned catastrophe, expensive drugs, hookers, close associates were all consumed- HK expat style...what evolved was a reliance on my career as a pro muso evolving to the point that I couldn't move back to oz cause I was making too much money and working so hard. Plus I liked the challenge of the gigs, mostly well-skilled musoz who could read music play just about anything without complaining, real Pros. Another issue of music in Hong Kong was that the locals like harmonious music no aggressive neurotic sounds here, took me a while to adapt, but with black music musoz and its romantic, funky vibe with jazzy chord progressions I very much enjoyed bathing in this aura. Performing most times with Afro Americans, skilled Philippinos, who by the way all exuded a joy & happiness in performance, different from the aggrorock driven gigs back in Oz, they also forged 'smooth' easy listening jazz to cater for local tastes (but you still needed pro skills of reading, harmony & improv plus groove!) and we got paid for our work including rehearsals etc. The scene circa 'handover' was busy & phenomenal! I arrived on the scene with my Aussie angular assertiveness, which btw never left me, however I settled into a pro musos life giving what needed.

Cats like me, Peter Scherr, Joe Rosenberg & Linus Y began performing our brands of jazz- free, harmolodic, Ornette, Braxton, NYC derived & all hell broke lose!:) Catherine Lau bless her from the Fringe Club HK agreed to put on our gigs. LKF and environs morphed into the most happening area , it was UNREAL!!!The downside is that Asian customers like to hang with Jazz n Wine- its perceived as high class & to maintain face they request songs, ordering booze for everyone-exerting their power & influence. Not joining in, results in a loss of face, if one has a liking to booze, one finds themselves an alchoholic quickly...However in hind sight after 10 years touring in bands in Oz, then migrating to HK to play the standard repertoire for 20 years, freelancing etc. 6 months prior to stroke I thought I had become master of guitar, but now I feel that at this point (after 40 years)I had found my own voice musicality/ voice, having taken in Jimi Hendrix, Miles, Coltrane, McLaughlin, Beck, valuable collaborations, unbelievable amount of gigs etc. now I was on point to present my music.

Kaboom Pow! STROKE!!! No mate.

Oz wouldn't allow me such as a self-employed muso shaping my own destiny. The horriblest fing is I remember how to play but I cant. Oz represented a lacklustre future coined by all the ocker trappings of boredom. Here in honky I was playing Jazz, seeing the world, shaping my destiny & becoming somewhat of an entrepreneur & contributing to the local music community, it was gregariously exciting!

The sadness I carried in my heart by moving to HK was that of leaving Dad all fucked up by a stroke in the nursing home "The Burlington" in Katoomba, (but we did manage to fly him up to HK for a couple of weeks) and Mum based in blue mountains, eventually it all played on my guilt & mental capacity.

But I had to do it for my kids & my sanity. Taking off from Charles Kingsford Smith on Vietnam Airlines bound for Hk via Saigon, we flew right over the top of Katoomba, tears rolled down my cheeks, and I proceeded to join my new onboard Aussie-Viet friends who were going back, in consuming the copious amounts of whiskey they provided.

I wasn't a good look when I finally stumbled into the arrivals hall at Kai Tak Airport HK, Sylvia already started to complain and nag. I lasted seven years living as a family in a flat the size of a matchbox in Sha Tin (a district not a place to poo). I could never seem to grasp Canto language as there had not been a logically thought out system to it's way of teaching, where as Mando had a very good system and logic, most expats like me, just picked up HK Canto phrases or sentences, like *"Yau Lok"* = get off ie: minibus or taxi, but we didn't know what *Yau* and *Lok* meant individually. This sort of thing would be the beginning of the frustration and hate that develops over time in HK. Duality again, one minute you hate the place, the next you love it, when you're away from it you miss it. Then you're back and can't wait to get away again...

> "And it seemed to him he was always homesick for some place which he had never known and perhaps would never know. He was always homesick for somewhere else. He always hated where he was silently but deeply." D.H. Lawrence's Boy in the Bush

Work-wise, there were a lot of opportunities, with Lan Kwai Fong and Wan Chai having numerous live music venues. Jazz was pretty popular. Right up my desired alley.

HK being Asia's hub also meant there were many events and functions to cater for, bringing in top dollar.

Additionally it was quite awesome to have visiting top international musos & be in the company of luminaries like Darryl Jones, Peter Bernstein, Larry Coryell, Martin Taylor, Georgie Fame, Guy Barker, Roy Hargrove, Stan Tracy, imported Blues musicians that played a residency, to name some. & the top Aussie Jazzers, each encounter spawning quite a story.

In the beginning of my time 2nd time in HK, I would rock along to venues and ask to sit in, which was quite acceptable as the resident musos were always on the look out for new talent. I was a pretty good guitarist, handing out my cards, and within weeks found I was accepting gig offers left right and centre. Primarily I worked 'Lan Kwai Fong' - *Jazz Club, Fringe club* (where I met my brother by another mother Robbin Harris), *Steps, Swing, Blue Door, Browns, Bruce Lee Café, Stauntons* and many others, in addition Wan Chai gigs *Mes Amis* (where *Zmen* maintained a residency for a year and many other venues I performed in. It was an ecstatic experience playing with mainly American cats (black and white), and so frequently, I felt like this HK was *the boom town*, like something in USA in the 1920's and 50s" as it prospered or London in the swingin 60s. It was a heady mix! I had never done so many freelance gigs, needless to say "no time for wanking (da fei gei) but my music kung fu was developing in leaps and bounds.

At points I really felt like I and other expat musoz were pioneering a jazz music pathway forward in gigantic China, I hoped that by the time I was 60, I may have a standing in China as an entrepreneur or professor. still working and performing at a top tier level. Alas dee stroken! Nein!

I think it's worthy to give a description of these two vibrant areas of Hong Kong...

Lan Kwai Fong

Basically owned and visualised by Mr. Alan Zemen (a.k.a Mr. Lan Kwai Fong) a Canadian Jew. Located on the hill behind Central CBD HK, starting from the top of Wyndham St. and D'Aguilar St with bars and restaurants lining each side, the street winds down the hill, presenting what google maps describes as "A lively dining night spot". A place to hang, meet, drink, score drugs, eat, pick up chicks, boys or whatever you fancy. The buzz in the 80's was undeniably overwhelming.

I once was applauding the great local jazzman/guitarist Eugene Pao, then realised I was sitting next to Robert Plant in the LKF Jazz Club owned by Alan Z. LKF was far more classy than Wan Chai. However the ole Wan Chai had it's points too (a drunken 5 mins cab ride down the hill).

Wan Chai

Where as Lan Kwai Fong contained mostly the "beautiful" people of HK, Wan Chai was more like Kings X, seedy and cheaper, if you wanted a hooker it would be cheaper here. In fact, pending your definition of "hooker", one could be found for free, with a price to be remunerated later:)

Horizontal Wan Chai basically runs down from the Police Headquarters down two level main streets - Jaffe Rd and Lockhart Rd. Travelling down these streets reveals numerous bars, restaurants and pubs, with the addition of some "girlie" bars packaged with a lovely looking SE asian girl in sexy gear and the mama-san standing outside - go inside and one is confronted with numerous lovelies hoping for you to buy them a drink or take them "out" to fuck them, with an exorbitant exit fee overseen by mama-san. Once inside, it's a joke compared to the X (Kings Cross), no nudity, just lame Filipinos or Thai's gyrating against a pole looking bored shitless. Until the one you wink at comes over and requests you buy her and yourself a drink. Many a time a tourist has been caught out with a ridiculous bill. As a local and ham sup lo, the move is to treat these lonely ladies courteously and get their phone number. After which you may get lucky.

In addition to the usual Wanchai activity of Monday to Saturday, Sunday (day off for domestic helpers) sees a flood of domestic helpers (like family support workers they are on call 24/6) arrive in the Chai, as that is their only day off. Besides WC, the local parks are inundated with these chattering Indo and Filipino birds. The pretty & game ones hit Wan Chai to "hookup". Expat males are on the look out also, it can be quite sickening at times to see a perfect SE Asian specimen on the arms of some fuckwit older ex-pat. But such is life in HK.

If Bruce Lee had a problem with Hollywood, then here in HK you observe a problem with humanity. It is certainly a drop-off point from Alien Spaceships. God is the Supreme Alien.

Hong Kong ~ Sai Kung (living out of the city) 2004-2014

It wasn't really until I settled solo a number of years later after three years in China and some time in Adelaide finally back in HK to stay in Sai Kung Country Park in Ko Tong Ha Yeung Village, here I settled into a monoality. I loved this spot. It was totes awesome, and to wake up with Sharp Peak hovering amongst majestic mountains with wildlife, roaming feral cows, snakes, monkeys, butterflies in a wild jungle, was a spectacular HK living experience. Seriously, often macaques would be swingin outside my bedroom window. In addition, Wong Shek Pier was only 15 mins down the road, which allowed one to hop on ferries to startling locations like Tap Mun Island and Shek Kong. It was beyond words!

Ritual...I bought a little Honda Civic as I was teaching a bit and only did student home visits. My kids never visited me there except just once where I showed them the water inlet where I had in a ritual, jumped in with Dad's ashes to send him off. I had been carrying around his ashes for yonks, in fact those ashes along with a Buddha statue were miraculously left in my van, when it was robbed by thieves in Adelaide. I was determined to put Dad to rest somewhere lovely. He loved the sea and sailing as a youngster, and mountains as he got older. So, one terribly drunken afternoon in Ko Tong Ha Yeung, the village I lived in Sai Kung Country Park, I grabbed the ashes

115

box I'd been carting everywhere and put on me cossies and went down to Tai Tan Bay which had sea and mountain, dived in the beautiful clear water, smothered dad on my face and body and said goodbye to him in my own little ritual, much like an Australian aboriginal dance with painted ashes, and swum around until we became one. This I showed the kids once, probably adding to their opinion of lunacy about me. "Chi Sin Gwai-Lo" – a common Canto phrase meaning *crazy foreigner!*

What they didn't understand was that I was stripped of my ability to usher them into a normal world. As we know here in Oz.

Ie. Music lessons or Art on a Saturday. Sport team activities on a Sunday, along with family time with all the rest of Oz benefits. Nowhere to be seen in HK on average wages, people & limited space...It is a different lifestyle. I was frustratingly unable to implement a replica to my kids of my /aussie youth.

I've taken my son Julien and Li Yin to dads ritual area. A lovely spot that I returned to with Julien to collect some of the water (& Dad) to take back to Oz and spread around the Leura Crematorium where we held Dad's funeral, I did this with Bellisa in ritual.

By this stage I have HK PR – citizenship status, having spent 7 years in Sha Tin and 3 years in China. Also spent some time getting the kids to have a decent education in Adelaide...I rescued them, as did my mother, their NanNan. Like all parents, I think they are special and quite awesome, I am love them. This is where and when I actually experienced life as a divorced immigrant however still pre stroke and living in a typical ex pat's bubble sustained by basing myself in Sai Kung, a district like a paradise, really and very unlike the predominant HK residential areas of high rise and urban chaos and connection. An example of this bubble begins with the trip on public transport to work. For the commute from Sai Kung village, you get the mini bus along Hiram's Highway which is a picturesque journey through little villages, lush greenery and huge mountains on the right (often with Paragliders hovering above) with the sparkling sea on the left. Terminating at Tsung Kwan O a designated satellite suburb. At the (TKO) MTR station we descend on an escalator below ground and stay there for the thirty minute ride to Central (CBD/downtown of HK and close to all the venues). When I settled in Ko Tong village deep in the Country Park, it was the same trip, add on the most spectacular 30 minute Wong Shek Pier number 94 bus ride.the 94 bus driver is a kind legend!

https://www.youtube.com/watch?v=OoM2OawPSgs

After the gig I would use a third of my pay for a direct taxi ride home (30kms one way) and wake up in wonderland the next day and do it all again. Eventually I bought a car and drove in and back adding to the bubble life, as most HK people don't have cars, they live in small cramped boxes and commute on dreary transport lines. It was somewhat of a charmed life, quite different from the locals. I felt somewhat removed from society and this allowed me to daydream and get creative. My mate up the road, Peter Scherr owned a very nice recording studio, and with mate rates I was able to document a lot of my music. I rented a small bachelor from a villager. Most of the indigenous village people had deserted their villages for life in the city, these villages offered some interesting locations for photos and exploring and plain old reminiscing, the country parks seriously offer an incredible glimpse of native countryside, truly amazing as opposed to the concrete shopping, residential & office clutter downtown. There wasn't much socialising (typical country village life fared) except with the Scherr's up the road or with the feral cows (the cows rallied around when I played tai chi). My main issues of being an immigrant in HK escalated when I lived in the dense urban concrete jungles & becoming a stroker! here an interesting notion may exist.

The hypothesis of linguistic relativity, part of relativism, also known as the Sapir–Whorf hypothesis, the Whorf hypothesis or Whorfianism is a principle claiming that the structure of a language affects its speakers world view or cognition, and thus peoples perceptions are relative to their spoken language. This may be a thing. Here in the country park life was beautiful. Not much kung fu training, when I did do my Tai Chi, the cows would rally around for a look. I began teaching guitar a fair bit to neighbours and going to students homes. Daniel Ng, Paul Chow and Dr. John Chung became my dedicated students along with Ron Ng later, teaching became a joy for me and another reasonable income source so I began to take it more seriously and decided to promote myself in this area of middle class residents.

After an emotional break up with Lisa Simis, I flung myself into the business of teaching and found myself signing a lease in Clearwater Bay to live solo & extend my teaching. Moving into a three story house in Clear Water Bay, another supremely beautiful district not far from Sai Kung but closer to the MTR and only a ten minute walk down a jungle track to the shopping area. Here I had a ready made list of local/close expat students as previously I had driven to their places to teach, but now they all agreed to come to my new music studio. Luke Riggs and Jack Bojan, both brilliant young British boys were way into it as were successful ex pats, Gary Seib and Jerry Smith who became top students also. Even though my rent had more than doubled, my income rose sharply as well as making savings on transport and most importantly - **time**.

I was living alone. Gigs were flowing. It seemed perfect but something was missing.

In hindsight,

HK blew my mind apart. Re- my kung fu music, I was in brotherly friendship with outstanding American musicians, people like Mr. Larry Hammond ('brothers keeper' alumni), my most favourite singer, (a drummer also) initiating me to Gap band and much popular black music I was unaware of. Mr. Allen Youngblood (another 'brothers keeper' alumni): band leader/pianist, exposing me to African Caribbean music from his hometown US Virgin Islands, Mr. Mark Henderson (trumpinitor) an incredible cat determined to continue the "hard-bop" movement and broad enough to work with open minded DJ's, who would spin, with me and Mark groovin' along.

I learnt the ropes from these amazing men, afterward meeting and collaborating with awesome bassists Mr. Flynn Adams (Kansas City) and the genius Mr. Peter Scherr (Massachusetts).

Basically I was a little whitey from Mosman Oz who had lived a year in North America when I was 16. I could play pretty well, and I had an open attitude along with respect & passion.

However, previously I had climbed the guitar ladder in Sydney/Oz. by creating a few awesome bands, *THEM OR US* and *PLAYDIEM*. In addition to touring the country for 10 years in Nationally famous bands, *EUROGLIDERS, IAN MOSS* and *MATT FINISH*. More in "My Kung Fu Music" www.mykungfu.com.au

So I wasn't some *nimno* having just arrived on the scene in HK.

I serviced Hong Kong, and Hong Kong serviced me. La

The **Chi** *[vital life energy]* should be excited, The **Shen** *[spirit of vitality]* should be internally gathered. The postures should be without tension.

I must say I enjoyed a very diverse & engaging professional career in music from 1970's right through to a Stroke in 2014. I elaborate more on it in my book – My kung Fu Music

Available here

Isbn: 978-0-6454336- 0-9

Here's a snippet …

…

MY KUNG FU Music One ~ Australia

In the old days 70s/ 80s in Sydney, there was a vibe. In my day as a novice performer – during the 1980's, I was again torn in a duality of pursuing Jazz vs. Rock/Pop. To be poor or earn some money was a factor too. A life dedicated to jazz through late teen years eyes didn't appear to result in 'being well off'. In the Oz pop scene we had a number of local bands creating wonderful music, **The Church, Icehouse, Matt Finish** and specific songs immersed themselves in one's consciousness like *Under the Milky Way, Short Note, Great Southern Land, Cheap Wine* ansd *Evie*. It may be ludicrous to say that **Midnight Oil, INXS** and **Cold Chisel** were the top three. I loved them. I'm talking 70's to 80's. With the Sydney jazz scene we had the *Paradise Jazz Cellar* – where you could hear the likes of **Dale Barlow, The Benders, Mark Simmonds Freeboppers, James Morrison, Steve Brien, Robbie Krupski** and **Roger Frampton**. At the *Criterion Hotel* you had **Joe "BeBop" Lane** and his loyal entourage, or check out **Crossfire** at *The Basement* and **Kerrie Biddel** at *The Soup Plus*. It was a vibrant and exciting era along with other pioneering outfits around the scene like **Stepps, Jupiter, Pyramid, Sounds from Earth, Ayers Rock, Espirito, Nebula** and **The Free Beer Band** all playing incredible music. Later there appeared Jackie Ozarski's Jump Back Jack/Hungarian Rapsadists & others.

Growing up in the 60's was subjected to boredom and restraint as Australia was quite an isolated parochial place that no one ever much came to, especially famous creative artists. I somehow knew I'd never see Jimi Hendrix live, then he died same with Bruce Lee, so when I saw the film *Jimi Plays Berkeley* (where I would later go) on the big screen at a special Rock screening in Manly and pumped through a *mother fucka* sound system, I freaked. After seeing him in motion, I knew that's what I wanted to do. As much as I had heard that some guitar geniuses couldn't read music or had no training. I thought differently. This attitude helped me big time in sustaining a professional music career.

Jimi Hendrix: The most incredible musician ever. Fucken' oath. Totes blew me away. When Miles met Jimi....*"Yo Miles, you alien mofo, welcome to my club, we are both blues musicians, we took it into outer space"* "*Yo Miles, I don't know if I can get into this modal shit*" said the free spirited Sagittarius to the moody Gemini. Therefore nothing happened. Miles Davis couldn't control it.

My next huge influence would be John McLaughlin, an Englishman and guitarist that exuded a gentlemanly aura of eastern mysticism and clean living, technical prowess as a musician, plus an introduction to **JAZZ**. Quite a different kettle of fish to Jimi who passed away at the age of 27. John, amazingly still performs and is in his late 70's. He is really my secret /silent Mentor. Later Joe Pass.

I loved Mosman and Mosman High School was a nurturing centre for music making.

Loved my school Mosman High, fellow students included Brett Border, brother of Australian Cricket Captain Allan. Comedian/Actor Paul Hogan's sons Clay, Brett and Todd, John Meillon's son John Jnr. Jim Frazier's (a respected natural wildlife cinamatographer)son Chris Frazier. Melissa Blanche whose mum Kiersten was an ABC producer. In addition it nurtured musicians such as Tony Buck (The Necks), Tom Ellard (Severed Heads) and myself. I had lots of interesting friends, and liked some of the teachers and subjects, I was always intrigued by scripture class, as I couldn't figure it all out and liked Asian Social Studies. Later in my life Asia and Buddhism would play a central role. Sometimes, I think we already know what's going to happen. John Biggers and Brett Curotta were a couple of my best friends, we loved music and surfing, Brett was probably the best surfer. This was our Kung Fu, we used to get up early to go surfing, a sort of North Steyne gang ensued with Doug Ironside, Anthony Weaver and others, we all stored our boards there at the Surf Shop, and Levi's were de rigeur. In music class initially we were all bored shitless with a classical repertoire. Later a new teacher with a beaut L series Stratocastercame onboard & encouraged us. We dug him... Macy, Dugald Brown, Simon Baderle, Dikran Balian, Rolf Knudsen, Chris, me and Tony Buck, Doug Ironside, Brett Curotta, Ralph Hague all began performing and a healthy dose of competition and comradeship developed. Repertoire consisted mainly of Hendrix, Pink

Floyd, Led Zeppelin, Santana. Along with originals. After my year in North America, I knew I wanted to be a full time musician. By this age at 18 I was really a beginner. I left school, got a job at Berny's Radio and with some income was able to afford lessons at the Academy of Guitar in Bondi. Two years of this and I came out infatuated with fusion and with a keen desire to pursue jazz and chase gigs. I had developed my rock guitar style to a satisfactory level. Through my practice and study I found new chords on the guitar until I understood their structure. It was so exciting that I could create my own chords and voicings. During my day job at Bernys Radio, I met Midnight Oil guitarist Jim Moginie, saxophonist Paul Andrews, befriended Greg Sheehan. Paul really introduced me to Coltrane in his funky crib down at Mosman Bay near my house. Greg was this magnetic, inspiring hippy percussionist dude who was part of the band *Sounds from Earth*.

I co-formed a few groups with Chris Frazier, Tim Lumsdaine and Tony Buck for little gigs around the place. When I got out of Berklee College Boston and finally landed back in oz around 1981, I attended the Sydney Conservatorium Summer Jazz Clinic. We had a Hal Galper class, with which in addition to the stint at Berklee, I understood the importance of forward motion in phrasing and rhythmic placement. As I now hoped to fuse hard driving rock with jazz heavy metal bebop. My study and the little time at Berklee, plus 9 hours practise a day, allowed me to tackle most musical situations. I immediately formed the "Guy Le Claire Quintet" with Steve Hunter (bass), Andrew Gander (drums), Jason Morphett (sax) and Kevin Hunt (piano/keys). An originals jazz group, we held a residency at "Jenny's Wine Bar" on Pitt St. I also recorded my stuff in the February of 1984.

https://guyleclaire.bandcamp.com/album/le-claire-quintet-rsvp-2

Now that I'm in my sixties, I can look back and see that my love affair with jazz didn't just begin with going to Berklee college of Music in Boston, it was sustained with the challenge the music presented and all the wonderful, interesting, knowledgeable cats committed to jazz & the music itself. Grandpa Jack was an avid jazz fan, having over a thousand jazz recordings, he also took Mum to see Satchmo and a host of others thanks to the philanthropist Adelaide Boynthon family, Patrons of Jazz.

In a way I came upon jazz back to front. Immersed in Miles from *In A Silent Way* onto John Coltrane's *I Love Sydney - A Love Supreme* actually. That changed somewhat at Berklee with a chance meeting and jam in the Massachusetts Ave basement rooms with Kevin Daley, a very fine guitarist. These went well and he kept inviting me to jams. Finally my *one key* aptitudes ran out on standards like *"All The Things You Are"* as Kevin ripped and I flopped big time.

By passion, insight and exploring the traditions of *Trad, Bebop* to knowing *the standards repertoire*, I morphed. Guitarists Mike Stern and John Scofield were huge influences. These two were already doing what I was thinking. I needed to learn it. Berklee gave me that impetus and direction.

Boxing day 26th December 2019...Listening to the Miles Davis box set I picked up in Lithgow. He finishes with his take on Cyndi Lauper's *Time after Time*, Fuck I miss that guy!. My plan was to get over to NY and join his band.

Band of Gypsy's *"Machine Gun"*, the be all and end all of electric guitar. *"Power of Soul"* Jimi is trying to encourage us *"with the power of soul, anything is possible"* or is that with the power of the Dole?

FB 1976

...Me and mum San Francisco. We're walking down the road in Berkeley CA and I see the place where Jimi Hendrix played/performed "Hendrix in the West" album & the gig that I saw in Manly theatre thru the pumping motha fucka sound system. His awesome rendition of Johnny. B Goode is going through my 16 year old mind. The footpath we're on, two gorgeous looking black chicks are approaching, Happy, they eye me off, smiling. My little willy is blushing...

By the mid 1980's, I was touring all over Australia in very well known bands *Eurogliders, Ian Moss Band, Matt Finish* and freelancing as a session muso plus teaching privately also. However, by the end of that decade I was burnt out. In search of respite, the family relocated to the Blue Mountains (100 km's west of Sydney). All of us including my Dad lived there which was good, Mum was already up there, however the arse had fallen out of the live music scene, and I worried about the mortgage. In 1991, I released my self titled debut GUY LE CLAIRE on CD independently and received some very good press from the media both domestically & international. As a result I was offered "Head of the guitar Department" at AIM (Australian Institute of Music) in Sydney. I then commuted 5 days week on the 2 hour train trip from Katoomba to Central. In all this I put some bands together. Faves being *Them Or Us* with Geoff Lungren and Bill Heckenberg, GleC and the *Frank Sonatas* with Chris Frazier, Warren Trout and Bill Risby, *Playdiem* with Steve Hunter, David Jones and John Foreman. *Zilch* mountain band with Boof, Gary Evans and Frank Corby. Having jazz guru & legend bassist, Blue Mountains resident Bruce Cale as a mentor enabled me to study and play with a real jazzer. In fact we got on so well as people and players, we ended up holding a weekend residency gig (Fri/Sat) as a jazz duo at the Hillcrest Coachman in Leura for two years, culminating in a Wangaratta Jazz appearance and a CD. With Bruce, the beauty for me was to get *outside of my head and play!* Just *play it!* That way it begins to internalise. This experience would set me up well for future gigs in HK.

I've had the good fortune of playing with many great Australian Musoz, such as Dale Barlow, Jonathan Zwartz, Matt McMahon, Hamish Stuart, Tim Bruer, Alex Hewetson, Paul Joseph, Paul Andrews, Sandy Evans, David Jones, Steve Hunter, John Fpreman, Chris Frazier, Warren Trout, Andrew Gander, Kevin Hunt, Jason Morphett, Peter Dehlsen, Jeremy Sawkins, Azo Bell, Tim Rollinson, John Prior, Lindsay Jehan, Kevin Borich, Dave Adams, Harry Brus, Rebecca Johnson, Rex Goh, Phil Witcher, Peter Northcote, Sam McNally, Steve Sowerby, John *'Watto'* Watson, Mark Kennedy, Armando Hurley, Mark Costa, Alan Dargin, Chong Lim, Don Reid, Mark Riley, Jan Preston, Gary Evans, Mina, Paul Najar, Justin Dileo, Maddy and Mick Young, Ian Belton, Steve Fearnley, Dave Colton, Stan Mobbs, Steve Prestwich, Will Scarlett, Mike Hague, Grace Knight, Bernie Lynch, Chris Sweeney, Steve Merta, Bob Wynyard, Dario Bortolin, Gordon Rytmeister and Dave Addis. The list is extensive though I may have missed some talent.

MY KUNG FU Music Two ~ Hong Kong

As I've mentioned earlier, hopping up on stage in HK to sit in with a band was not frowned upon, in many ways it was welcomed. It broke the monotony of HK gigdom and the musoz were interested to hear what you did. So armed with new business cards, I jumped up wherever possible and that my friends led to many gig offers. I got very busy pretty quickly.

All my Aussie pro gig experience helped me in business and dealings with musicians. I formed the first of many bands here, the Guy Le Claire Trio with Peter Scherr on double bass and Anthony Fernandes on drums. We recorded our gig at the HK Jazz Club and I released it independently. That CD was well received and placed me into some media spotlight and inherent local musical gossip. More and more gigs came, sometimes three a day, this lasted more than 2 decades playing with luminaries Allen Youngblood, Justin Siu, Blaine Whittaker, Mark Henderson, Flynn Adams, Eugene Pao, Larry Hammond, Peter Scherr, Elaine Liu, Johnny Fuego, Gemma & Jondi Mac, Ted Lo, Bob Mocarsky, Rickard Malmsten, Paul Candelaria, Jnr Carpio and Johnny, Skip Moy, Sylvain Gagnon, Oliver Smith(le French trio not from France/*muaarggghhh*) and fulfilling Jazz Club residencies performing with imported American Blues acts such as Phil Guy, Guitar Shorty, Eddie King and Luther Guitar Junior Johnson to name some...

By the early 2000's I was touring world-wide with HK pop stars (Canto/Mando pop). These were high paying/level reading gigs, luckily my reading had blossomed but the tricky rhythmic phrases on paper were doing my head in. I diverted to Konokol, the traditional Indian music science and found that the tricky semi quavers were singable therefore playable. These gigs paid well there was a lot of pressure. There was no time for kung fu training.

Worth a mention was the blossoming of an area called Soho, sandwiched between mid-levels and Sai Ying Pun focussed along Hollywood road, here blossomed a number of new music venues we all played in. Le Rideux run by Frenchman Christophe Bonno(he also ran 'Geckos'), beneath was the Aqua restaurant where I oversaw the music program - md, & over to the happening Peel street, featuring 'Peel Fresco', with 'Joyce is not here', upwards to the Makumba African Bar all with live music 7 nights a week – darn it was a hang!

As was my routine, I completed my usual cycle of *work hard - burn out - retire to get energy back*. In an attempt to break this cycle, I settled in Clearwater Bay closer to the city to help slow my performance rate down as I was looking to build my private teaching business up. Along with very enjoyable teaching sessions with top students Ron Ng, Daniel Ng (no direct relations) along with Gary and Jerry (who all helped me immensely post stroke) and Luke Riggs, Jack Bojan, brothers Saxon and Jarvis Whittaker, I began enjoying the teaching process and the little business prospered.

I must say it was a joy to be playing alongside great HK musoz as mentioned previously - adding to that list: Jason Ho, Skip Moy, Rudy Balbuena, Dodong Fuego, Joey Villanueva, Paul Candelaria, Justin Siu, ChoiA Kun, Anthony Leung, Roel Garcia, DC, Paul Levi, Mark Peter, Tom Tse, Siraj, John Von Seggern, Jun Kung, Angelita Li, Jezreal Lucero, Sidwell O Neil, Joe Rosenberg, Steve Sacks, ABA, Kai Djuric, Ginger Kwan, Donald Ashley, Tommy Ho, Tsang Tak Hong, Jondi Mac, Benjamin Li, Joyce Peng, Gaz Selb, Jez Smith, Mike Carr, Balu, Gary Da Silva, Oz Walker, Franklin Torres, Tom Nunan, Jim Schneider, Michelle Carillo, Dan LaVelle, Brigitte Mitchell, LeLe, Zhang Zhi Yong, Ted Lo, Rob Scott, The Carpios, Yip Dak Han, Tsai Qin, Sally and George Lam, Faye Wong, Peter Lee, Joao Mascaranhas, Chinda, Scotty Wright, Miles Li, Kenny Matsura, Jason Cheng, Mano Manolette, Wink Vastine Pettis, Charlie Huntley, Chris Polanco, Joel Haggard, Dave Packer, Dale Wilson, Cary Abrahams, Jamie Murcell, Melchoir, The Aranas, Chris Collins, Les Fong, Jeff Young, Bob Mocarsky, Ray Covington, Nicholas McBride, Nicholas Bouloukos, Gilbert Caselis, Michael Wong, David Tong, Charlie Foldesh, Howard McCrary, Mike Carr, Stephen Ives, Tim Wilson, Winnie Chung, Sybil Thomas, Manuela Lo, Pierre Veniot, Pete Kelly, Neil Irwin plus *all* the musoz who played in my bands or I played with in their bands...Afro-Cuba run by Mark Henderson & Mano Manolette was memorable.

?Buybee arrived from London with his bag of vinyl & high hopes of rockin out in hk/ quickly after hangin out in lan kwai fong and soho, Buybee gets a gig as a dj. Hk blew his mind, walking 24/7 he found pockets of every Asian culture open, spunk filipinas, indoz, chinese and british guys & girls kept him busy & de food! little pockets of communities & pubs, with all races of expat musicians he could converse with. Buyby fell in love with HK & became the dj spokesman for HK with its new trendy sexual preference agenda. Unt das vas dee ent of das!?

Banff Centre for the Arts 2001– both as a jazz course participant & artist-in-residence.

Banff exposed me to high art jazz music. Living with progressive musicians, teachers & mentors Dave Douglas, Kenny Werner, Jim Black, Peter Knight, Michael Bates, Joe Lovano, Judi Silvano, Fiona Burnett, Alex Tsiboulski allowed me to switch on to a whole new area in music that I had actually been thinking about. Here I got the encouragement & support. We recorded some interesting music.'C' check it out, I lugged all my Chinese instruments over.

https://soundcloud.com/guy-le-claire

FB

...Aussie musos are recruited by me in HK, or if they are passing through, I set up gigs for Dale Barlow, Simon Barker, Steve Hunter, Scott Tinkler, brother Chris Frazier, Tony Buck, Peter Knight, Scott Tinkler and Andy Gander...

Everything ended with the *Stroke*. I sold the studio stuff and all the guitars, amps etc. to survive. Couldn't pay storage and lost it all. Diu! Fucken Diu Lei Lo Mo!

FB

...Listening to John Lee Hooker's *"One Beer, One Scotch, One Bourbon"* has me remembering aussie muso Peter Kekel. *Tequila Slammers* on the Will Scarlet gig.... At FCC in HK with Allen Youngblood sometimes we would have a beer and scotch...

In my musical career, I had the energy to form a number of bands, not in chronology, only as I remember

Guy Le Claire Quintet ~ Steve Hunter, Jason Morphett, Andy Gander, Kevin Hunt.

Guy Le Claire and the Frank Sonatas ~ Chris Frazier, Warren Trout, Bill Risby.

Guy Le Claire Trio ~ Peter Scherr, Anthony Fernandes.

Guy Le Claire Trio 2 ~ Scott Dodd, Robbin Harris.

Z-MEN ~ Robbin Harris and Flynn Adams.

Bruce Cale with Guy Le Claire ~ Duo

Zilch ~ Gary Evans, Frank Corby, Boof – Ray Husband

Guy Le Claire ~ John Prior, Lindsay Jehan.

Alchemy ~ Linus Why, Robbin Harris, Jondi Mac, Mark Henderson.

World Project ~ Tom Tse, Siraj, Cameron Reid, Sylvain Gagnon, Zhang Zhi Yong.

Playdiem ~ David Jones, Steve Hunter, John Foreman.

RED ~ Peter Scherr, Andrew Collier.

World Project – Sylvain Gagnon, Cameron Reid, Blaine Whitaker, Zhang Zhi Yong, Tom Tse, Siraj

Compadres ~ Esteban Antonio and Guy Le Claire duo.

FUNFF ~ Blaine Whittaker, Robbin Harris, Sebastien Meyer.

Them Or Us ~ Geoff Lungren, Bill Heckenberg.

I adored all theses bands and personnel.

Selected Discography:

* Guy Le Claire Quintet: RSVP 1984 (Cassette only Release)* Playdiem - Playdiem (Larriikin LRJ 329) 1994 CD * Guy Le Claire (GLC 001) 1991 CD (Out of Print)* Guy Le Claire Trio Live (3-logic-music 003) 1997 CD (Out of Print) * Guy Le Claire - Plonk (GLC 005) 1999 CD (Out of Print)

* Guy Le Claire & Bruce Cale –Standard Time 2002 CD(Out of Print) * Guy Le Claire - Xin Xin Solo 2002 CD (Out of Print) * Guy Le Claire - Red

(3-logic-music 007) 2003 CD (Out of Print) * Z-Men - Z-MEN 2003 CD (Out of Print)

* Guy Le Claire ROCK HITZ (3-logic-music 010) 2013 * Guy Le Claire Trio 2 (3-logic-music 009) 2013 CD * Guy Le Claire Solo 3 (3-logic-music 011) 2013 CD

2 CDs are currently available to buy and download:

from Amazon or eBay.

Guy Le Claire ~ *Solo 3* Guy Le Claire ~ *Trio 2*

most of it is on

bb youtube

Or go to the web address below for mp3's of most of the above selections and more.

https://guyleclaire.bandcamp.com/

more memories...

LATER DAYS Post *Stroke* life Australia

2015: I have returned to my country after nearly 30 years and as a disablederer. Poo ee.

"The secret of Aikido is not in how you move your feet, it is how you move your mind. I'm not teaching you martial techniques, I'm teaching you nonviolence... If all you think about is winning, you will in fact lose everything. Know that you and your opponents are treading the same path. Envelope adversaries with love, entrust yourself to the natural flow of things, unify Ki (Qi-Chi), body and mind, and efface the boundary between self and other. This opens unlimited possibilities...

...Those who are enlightened to these principles are always victorious. Winning without contending is true victory, a victory over oneself, a victory swift and sure. Victory is to harmonize self and other, to link yourself to the Divine, to yoke yourself to Divine Love, to become the universe itself."

MORIHEI UESHIBA, founder of Aikido.

AUSTRALIA

1st of all I would like to say thank you to Australia! All you Australians are seriously awesome, agreeeing to a social services system, ndis. Paying your taxable income & supporting us disableds. Thank you also to the 1st nations people of Australia! Darn A Lucky Country. Thank You so very deeply from my core thank you! I love Australia & the kind caring compassionate Aussies thanks again xxx

on another note.. people here are in constant need of scamming, getting funds from de government! Going on & on with claims, compensations etc. Enough is enough. What the Fuck are youz gonna do when the money runs out!? Think please. Aussie is full of scammers, con artists. Fuck I wanna live OS. 2023.

conclusively. The need to scam is a bit much for this old man, perhaps it's a human thing?

Adelaide 17th December 2015 return.

Coming home as a Sydney born & bred boy on SQ Air to my country of birth and landing in Adelaide where my Mum lives. Naturally I'm going to live with Mum, I am pretty much flat broke, she offered. Immediately set off to Centrelink and get put on Newstart (like a dole), I'm hoping I can get on the disability support pension(which was easy to obtain in hk), disability pension is a better rate, with more care and a prospect of independence. About 8 months later after a lot of fucking around, I receive it. Mum and I hash out a boarding deal/price.

Adelaide

My connection to Adelaide began with the settling of my mothers family there having migrated from the UK in the 50's. As a kid I often visited Grandpa, flying from Syd - Ado and on other occasions training it with mum & once on the ship the "Marconi", I was always stoked to go there. Grandpa was a kind big guy, with a fatherly affection. I lived here from 2015-17 it was the 1st place in Oz I lived in post stroke.

Adelaide: Australia's Undiscovered Gem...

Scratch the surface of Australia's undiscovered gem with its blend of wonderful beaches, wide boulevards and extensive parklands including the Adelaide Botanic Garden. The City of Churches chimes to the beat during festival season with the Adelaide Festival of Arts, Adelaide Fringe and WOMADelaide.

The River Torrens flows through the city from the surrounding Mount Lofty Ranges. The Adelaide Hills features The Cleland Conservation Park that includes a wildlife park where you can pat koalas and Mount Lofty Summit with its panoramic views of the city. Hahndorf, with its German history, is another highlight. The coast has some fantastic beaches. Historic Glenelg is Adelaide's favourite local playground and further south are the wide open shores of Aldinga where you can drive your car on to the beach.

There are few better multicultural markets than the Adelaide Central Market or choose from a host of marvelous museums and art galleries, some having free entry. The picturesque and historic Adelaide Oval is a favourite for sports lovers.

I was so excited to be back in Australia that I ended up in the Royal Adelaide Hospital with severe AF. I underwent my second cardioversion, which failed, until they changed my medication from *metropolol* to *sotalol*, then the ole heart went back to *sinus rhythm*. Adelaide is a lovely little city, with grand buildings and churches, and the River Torrens winding near the city then on down to the Gulf of St. Vincent which houses beautiful beaches from Glenelg to Henley (my favourite). Thirty minutes from here you could be up in the Adelaide Hills, a lovely area that can rival the Blue Mountains. Mum's place sits at the bottom of the Hills, only 15 mins by bus to the City, one could whiz up to Stirling or Blackwood in the Hills in no time, or Hahndorf a bit further. We used to have drives up to the Hills and later at Stirling markets, met Derek the plant man who loved mum's creations. Mum's residence includes a shop, which she opens weekends selling her fashion & creations and it became my job on Saturdays to run it. She continues with her creative work of producing contemporary clothes. Even though I am back in Australia, I continue my Kung Fu and pathway to recovery.

I am researching a lot of things and have become part of the Adelaide Soka Gakkai (Nichiren Buddhism) community, chanting daily.

Boxing Day: 26th December 2015

Boxing: What a kung fu! Cardio work out, Punching, Groundwork, Defence work, bobbing and ducking. I can't really do it, but I fantasise.

FB ...Felizardo Intervalo from Manila was my kung fu mate at Mosman High School, he had the Bruce Lee moves down to a tee... Studying videos of Muhammad Ali Basic strikes – jab, cross, hook, uppercut, crosses. Love it. And as it stands with Coreeda - Australian Aboriginal Wrestling.

If I was wrestled, I wouldn't have a clue what to do. I may be able to fly them away with Ging Tai Chi but if they got me in a lock I could be fucked, obviously wrestlers use their weight you don't need to be extra smart on that. Sifu Dennis (the ex hk cop) Modern Method & Harry Lok tried to get me to understand locks & anti locking, but with no mats on the floor (another typical HK fuck up) who'd wanna push it? Scania was the kid! It seems my Australian path is set. My research shows me that wrestling was the earliest of martial arts such as Shuai Jiao (China), Ancient African and Egyptian wrestling systems, and mostly Prankration from Greece, mixing wrestling with boxing. When I think about it, as a kid a lot of fights were wrestling based. As the temper was lost one would fling oneself onto the other, to pull them down- and then what? Try to hit them while down?, if the opponent knew how to wrestle, manipulate weight or lock you'd be fucked, panting and puffing until you scream "I give up! La!!".So Pankration obviously is a victorious stlye, the boxing part is believed to have developed in Sumeria. So there is the hypothesis of Alien / All originating in Africa, and moving East... following the Sun, the almighty power of all Aliens and beings.

"Regardless of whether you are in the northern or southern hemisphere, the sun will always rise in the east and set in the west."

"The Way of the Warrior has been misunderstood. It is not a means to kill and destroy others. Those who seek to compete and better one another are making a terrible mistake. To smash, injure, or destroy is the worst thing a human being can do. The real Way of a Warrior is to prevent such slaughter – it is the Art of Peace, the power of love." Morihei Ueshiba. *Aikido ju-jutsu.*

Australia is such an amazing place, made up of many immigrants, that have shaped today's country. Apart from acknowledging the indigenous aboriginal Australians, the peoples that immigrated & contributed notably are Italians, Greeks, Lebanese, Arabs, Brits, Islanders, Western Europeans, SE Asians, Chinese, Indians, Eastern Europeans, Africans creating communities, & the Jewish community. All have respect & love for their fellows. Here is quite harmonious. You are all magnificent!

4th March 2016

At Aikido late, watching the class from sideline, I see a lot of similarities between it and Zhaobao king tai chi, weight and waist manoeuvring, using weight to control opponent, pivoting hips, using smaller circles, not big movements. Peter Noble Sensei is good. With mats on the floor and safety, the students are able to safely practise the throws etc. there are methods to landing i.e. slapping the floor with your arms and hands (lessens impact) as well as crossing the feet/legs when rolling or somersaulting, a few times I have performed these to save me from a fall. .Small, compact movements of transferring weight. Keeping the arms tight and locked. It is not a very casual environment, rules, regulations and discipline are at the core. Rules: the attackers are close to the shrine, while the receivers are at the other end. Bowing and respect is of paramount importance done after each little segment of activity."Hanmi" is the basic stance and a rectangular stance was introduced today when standing behind opponent, weight is equally distributed on both feet, sitting on the floor cross legged or in meditation pose is maintained whilst receiving instructions. Finishing with Two claps at the end and 'arigato'. The Japanese way is alien to me.

'WHAT DO YOU MEAN BY kung fu? Kung Fu is a skill' I know dickhead. After a chat with Peter sensei, the Singaporean man made it known to me that he was 70 yrs old and a dedicated practitioner of Aikido, for a good long period. I decided I didn't really like him as he probably didn't like me.

A few days ago I was sent to Adelaide Cardiology for a heart scan/ echo - we discovered that my AF has gone, boy that was such good news! My medication is the same but now with the addition of Eleva, a pill to alleviate depression, not that I feel depressed, but mum thought I may need something to alleviate my excitement and anxiousness.

6th March 2016

My son Julien just took me out for Yum Cha in Adelaide Chinatown. This morning I attended the March inaugural SGIA (Soka Gakkai Australia) Adelaide meeting and Tracy told a funny story about being involved in the moment, not just going into automatic the "meatballs", happy to see Vipan, Vinayaka, Rajeev, Eric, Rahul and Sam. Now I'm at the badminton SA Club at Lockleys, my son has dedicated a good portion of his life to this game/skill, he is a state coach, he's working with 2 little kids, I can see he definitely has the skill to fire good shots back. Looking at the more mature players and all the players, there is a vital need to hone reflex actions as the shuttlecock is unpredictable, soft to powerful rebounds are ways of winning, much like martial art!.

FB Mexico 1976

...after being stuck in Veracruz, it was with high spirits that Mum, Eddy and I headed for the Yucatan, home of Mayan Ruins. After bypassing Merida, we found Chichen Itza but settled on Tulum on the northern coast. This was a most idyllic location, and I think the lost photo of me here standing on a ruin with the beaches and glistening sea in the background was maybe a snapshot of the happiest and healthiest I ever would be. Considering I was in the bosom of Mayan Culture, eating and sleeping right, dipping into the sea daily & with Dad and the Australian Domestic scene thousands of miles away on the other side of the earth really...seemed unreal.

SURFING kung fu.

Surfing was my life and a kind of Kung Fu for me/us – North Steyne gang from the age of 13 to 17 I was totes engrossed in surfing.

All of one's particular Kung Fu is a passion and lifestyle and Surfing was it for me and many other young Aussies. The thing about our kung fuz is they are like religions, we are totally into it, dedicated followers, passionate.

Regain your optimism, do stuff! Don't willy wank around! You can do something – TRY IT.

I'll never forget when in a surf house cinema I saw Barry Kanaiapuni BK get thrashed on by the huge wave at Sunset, only to come exploding out with a massive powerful bottom turn & on to cruise the rest of the wave. Needless to say I was one proud teenager when I got my McCoy BK swallow-tail surfboard from mate Brett Curotta. Brett was a goofy footer like me and surfed really well. Anthony Weaver, possibly one of the most popular kids at school looked very natural in the water, he paddled well and moved his board around commandeeringly.

Out in the water today at Henley, ado, I seriously contemplated buying a board, after a few flashes of imagining riding a wave, then trying to stand up on the body board, I shelved that idea completely, a spaz surfing? I think not. In my own brain injured way I decided to do the Ukemis' front roll & back roll of Aikido in the shallow water/safe: As a true blue, and getting rather brown-skinned from the hot south Australian sun, I began to feel like a surfer again.

The North Steyne (Manly) gang of 1975 were mainly Mosmanites consisting of the Weavers, John Biggers, Doug Ironside, Rolf Knudsen, Brett Curotta, Stuart Brindle, Philip Blair and me of course. We hit the Steyne at every opportunity. Older Twizzle (goofy footer) was like the Lord, an extremely good surfer who could surf anything really well. A guy we all respected. To get down there we all often hitched, and a good bunch of "out" stories evolved from that experience, like once me & Doug got a ride and the guy pulled his cock out to start wanking... at the first set of red lights we jumped out & bolted, or in a hippie surfers VW van we got stuck at the Spit as the bridge was up and the dude pulled out a fat joint and says "you want some?" we chimed "yeh". By the time we got out at Spit Junction, I was so fucking high & out of it I couldn't figure about going home and facing my Dad (who was very straight).

Surfing fizzled out as life's sways pulled me to other regions i.e. Music, guitar and Working. I've just finished an engaging book by William Finnegan about his surfing life, I related to all of it. 'With music, as with waves, you are yielding to something more powerful than yourself." He doesn't mind if you call surfing *nuts*, just don't call it a sport. "It's an addiction. It can take over your life." 2023 I've just watched Gerry Lopez 'Yin Yang' movie, wah that brought back memories what a great guy :) Barry

Kanaiupuni, Nat Young, Midget Farely, Wayne Bartholomew, Jeff Hackman, Mark Richards all kung fu masters. To surf we all learnt by observation & Experimentation. No actual lessons. Bob McTavish 'surfing is an art. Sport can be measured, but art cannot.'

In memoramdum of Anthony Weaver,

SKIING kung fu.

With Dad we went to Thredbo to ski with Alliance Francaise de Sydney and after that episode we were both hooked on skiing, bloody expensive though unlike surfing ga la! Jean Claude Killy and Spider Sabich, later Ingemar Stenmark and Italian Alberto Tomba. There began my purchasing of ski magazines etc. (not to mention all the surf mags before) and love of skiing. I became a follower and "Thredbo-ite" my surf and school mate John Biggers was a Perisher dude and good skier, we began hanging and finally skiing together. John was darn good and always pushed me, we were Vedlynning down Crackenback once showing off and sending up beginners, like true surfies.

John eventually settled in Crested Butte, Colorado and has been a pro skier ever since. Darn I'd love to see him again! This is where the idea of leaving Australia may have begun, there was always this notion of time spent in the UK, meant that that 'Australian' was legit, I spent my time in Asia equalling non-legit time- from what I can see. My book doesn't have opportunity. Skiers wanted to go Europe & North America to chase good skiing conditions, surfers too Hawaii, Indo etc. there was always this spectacle that the 'thing' was overseas, we didn't see the value of our home soil. DERR.

Oz ski seasons were fraught with frightful conditions compared to Europe and North America, bad snow and reports along with short runs/mountain trails. Eventually I got to ski the OS ones, like when I landed in Calgary, Canada to go to the Banff Centre for Arts in Banff in 2001. The bus ride from the airport to Banff revealed snow-ridden Rocky Mountains. When I got to the Centre's reception on the Sunday arvo after flying from HK. The first thing I asked was "is there any skiing?" They said "today was the last day, but as the conditions are so good they (Sunshine) have extended another day". Class was due to begin the next day, Monday, I easily decided that I'll be skiing never the less, so early Monday morning I'm at Sunshine base getting all the gear, hop on the quad to the snow line, and can't believe how much snow there is.

Finally get to the summit tip the front of my skis over the fall-line and push off. Swish straight into my parallel turns carving down the mountain (I hadn't skied for over 10 years), getting on the triple chair back up I kept telling my Canadian counterparts how amazing this is to be in the Rockies amongst all this snow, as yesterday I was in Hong Kong, and that my friends is a *different world*!!!! Well after a good day skiing, I get back to my room that I am sharing with Peter Knight (a wonderful musician from Melbourne) and I can see the red message light on our phone blinking so I pick it up to retrieve the message from Sylvia *"Guy your Dad passed away this morning"* I was floored and confused as I knew I couldn't get back to the Blue Mountains quickly and had paid for this special 2 week course at Banff 2001. Dad had always told me that his father was put in the town's Pub Fridge (I visited this pub in Gladstone '22), so I knew Dad would at least be put in a preserved state. So I decided to continue with the three week course, it was a hard decision to make and a difficult time to get through. My method was to cycle as much as possible, weekends I was on the Banff - Canmore track (20 ks) I was totes paranoid and scared of confronting a bear out there in the wilderness, nature connected me to Dad.

Eventually we all meet up, Sylvia, Mum, Julien, Stassy and close friends converge at Leura Crematorium in the Blue Mountains and conduct a funeral service to honour my dear Dad on June 13th 2001.

To sum up my surfing spiel

Us surfers can remember well when we first started out, falling off all the time swimming in to retrieve your board (no leg ropes!) carving a beautiful bottom turn or cutback, getting in the tube! Heavenly, we were all self taught, our peers were our models, while paddling out it was a real buzz to see your mate do some good surfing on a wave. There was lots of natural camaraderie albeit an element of competition! Occasionally there were territorial issues but real surfers never fought each other.

In fact I remember a tai chi master stated in California that he felt the most natural students of his were surfers. As a surfer, we inherently were at one with the universe/the ocean (good song ay?) Yin/ Yang - the universe was part of our lives in the most natural way, the ocean/sea is yin yang, so how natural was it for me to gravitate to other kung fu skills and paths. William Finnegan thinks *all* good surfers start before they're 14yrs old, *"After that it's too late to be any good"*. My mum said today *"it's like you are going backwards in age, with this brain injury"* today at the beach I was a kid again. Will my brain rewire itself back to normal?

Music, Sex, Drugs and Rock'n'Roll, were all part and parcel of surf culture back in the 70's. My first drag of a smoke was at the beach 'cause surfers are aiming at being the coolest cats... It's all a pseudo brain-wash wank. What is cool, is in. What isn't, is out, there are some people that don't care about this and some that overly do. Being in rock bands or having a spunky girlfriend was cool. Money wasn't a big issue then when compared with the youth of today as far as I can see.

I thank Nichiren Buddhism for guiding me to an element of freedom.

Shower in the garden time!

Darn it feels great after that, I almost feel totes normal! So Hot! Like Haruki Murakami, I seem to be in the disgusting habit of smoking, then writing, Haruki smoked and ran, he finally knew he had to stop and he did! I indulge in time slots.

As I mentioned earlier, Bruce Lee can be considered the father of MMA (Mixed Martial Arts) I first heard of Royce Gracie (Brazilian Jiu Jitsu) from my brother Robbin and Canadian author of "Bruce Lee and Me". Seeking out Royce via youtube clips, I found a situation of grappling, and what looks a bit like wrestling on the floor/canvas - this intrigued me as I remembered some early school fights when the opponent overcame me by wrestling and strength I felt totally unable to resist, Royce in one of his last UFC fights takes on a massively muscly looking dude, and wins. This had me question the plight of Sifu's body momentum. It looked to me like, with body mechanics and skill one could even be overcome on the floor, quite a feat! Gracie has my respect.

One of the hardest punches I've ever seen is the *Systema* side punch, so it was with interest that I watched Tyson Fury vs Wladimir Klitschko. Both

Boxing champs, Fury is a tricky opponent and Vlad worked hard, no evidence of Systema but they both look like they can throw a mean weighted punch, both of them were lucky to duck some flyers. I used a systema punch into a wall and man! Did I make a hole.

27th December 2015 adelaide

After a lovely Christmas Day with my Mum (the first in ages), and hearing about a post Xmas day sale rush on at shops in the city, I decided to do some research on what kung fu may be on offer here in Adelaide. I've found a number of Wing Tsun schools the ole Jim Fung school, who has passed away, and a "Grandmaster" Leong , as well as Master Allan Kelson of Tai Chi Aus/Adelaide and some smaller individuals, who have national accreditation (?). Jeet Kune Do and finally, Adelaide Systema, which I am trying to get in touch with. I first heard of this method, from my drummer mate Nicholas McBride, who lives in Shanghai, he was urging me to seek it out.

2nd January 2016

Went downtown after a bit of an altercation with my mum. Seems I can't keep anyone happy in this state. Looking through the disability claim forms, with so many questions and stuff makes me feel like an unsuccessful candidate, I get confused. But yesterday I went to the New Years Daimoku Adelaide Soka Gakkai group, with Sam and his lovely wife Nori, Ashley and Vin, Chris, Eric, Ted, Wing, Elisabeth. Was nice to chant again, truly if you haven't chanted, try it!!! Better with other practitioners. While downtown I tried to seek out Chan from Capoeira, no luck but found Sifu Leong in Hindley St. He was a lovely jovial nice guy, we chatted a bit in Chinese. He said *"Tai Chi is medicine"*, he is Yip Man Athletic Ving Tsun 001 -1. He highly advised me to have Acupuncture with him. On going down the stairway from his big gym, that was nearly gutted out by fire. I found myself in a TCM clinic and had a free consultation with Dr. Wang Yisi. She didn't say much as I enthusiastically bumbled my way through Mando and Canto, but was interested to hear that I used my Tai Ji and Qi Gong to help repair myself. She stressed that since I know about Qi Gong and exercises, I should pursue this rigorously. Use the Qi Gong and exercise to get Qi and blood flowing, it will repair my crook shoulder.

There are two parks nearby here, Glenunga Reserve and Ridge Park, both are totally awesome, I need to get into them and I do, admittedly it's HOT.

Reading "Kung Fu Warrior - Way of Applied Wing Chun" Danny Leung. "if you don't know kung fu, how can you have confidence to fight a much bigger and stronger adversary?" - Wing Chun Warrior pge 66.

Having finished reading Melbourne lady Doris Brett's *The Twelfth Raven*, I thought I might quote some of it... *"Having been plunged into the role of carer for the very ill, hospitalized patient, I was horrified on a daily basis by the need of my role as patient advocate. Apart from researching the cutting edge developments in the field, I had the daily tasks of helping to make Martin (her stroke ridden hubby) life in hospital more comfortable, communicating with specialists and therapists to make sure they had the correct current information on Martins' state, making decisions when different options were offered, deciding on the need for second or third options- the list goes on. It is horrifying to imagine as helpless as one is in the wake of a stroke or other serious illness and not have anyone to do that research, advocacy and coaching on your behalf. It is a crucial part of recovery and both Martin and I are certain he would not have had the recovery he had without my input."*

11th January 2016 ado

Just got back from the city after banking my medibank cheque, damn getting low on money... reading / studying Bruce Lee, which naturally brings me to Ving Tsun. I Finished the book by Duncan Leung Sifu "Wing Chun Warrior" with some great quotes in there, especially the ones regarding the respect and fairness of Aussies.

12th January 2016

Yesterday David Bowie passed on, I never met David but in Rushcutters bay I knew he was nearby snorting.

Bruce Lee said, *"Martial Art is the expression of the human body... ultimately Martial Art means honestly expressing yourself"*

Jeet - *intercept/stop*, **Kune** - *fist*. **Do** - *way* - *way* of the intercepting fist. Created by Bruce Lee in HKG 1967.

Kalari Payattu, ancient healing and martial art in Southern India, banned by the British in 1804. Along with **Shaster Vidiya**, both awesome alien arts. Early kung fu.

Daisaku Ikeda "Time is equally given to everyone. Therefore being able to build a life of glory, victory and happiness depends on whether you spend your time meaningfully and free of regrets".

Mental Health Australia

Figures in The 2007 National Survey of Mental Health and Wellbeing, has found that one in five of Australian adults have had a mental disorder in the previous 12 months and that almost half the total Australian population would experience a mental disorder at some time in their lives. However, the prevalence of mental disorders declines with age, from 1 in 4 young people (16yrs - 24yrs) to 1 in 20 (75yrs - 85yrs).

Some of the main groups of Mental Disorders are: Mood Disorders (such as depression or bipolar disorder), Anxiety Disorders, Personality Disorders, Psychotic Disorders (such as schizophrenia), Eating Disorders, Trauma-related disorders (such as post-traumatic stress disorder *PTSD*) and Substance abuse disorders.

The diagnosis of mental illness can be controversial. There have been many debates in the medical community about what is and isn't a mental illness. The definition can be influenced by our society and culture, but most mental illnesses occur across all countries and cultures. This suggests that they are not just constructed by social norms and expectations, but have a biological and psychological basis too. Drug abuse can affect the lives of those caught up in it in ways they might not expect. From healthdirect.gov.au... 'when someone with a mental illness is called dangerous, crazy, or incompetent rather than unwell, it is an example of stigma. People with mental illness may face stigma – they may be viewed in a negative way, treated differently, and made to feel ashamed or worthless, as if they are less than other people. I feel octo-polar & heavily ptsd'd from youth parental breakup (I believe now I bottled it up) & the stroke amounted to a stress disorder! It's bloody hard work to maintain some equilibrium, especially with prick family around.

Sufferers may encounter affected health, relationships, jobs and education – sounds like strokers & disableds issues. Recognising there is a problem with drugs is an important first step in seeking help and treatment. Drug addiction can be treated, but it's important that the person using drugs seeks help and support to figure next steps, rather than trying to deal with it on their own. Drug abuse is often associated with illicit drugs such as speed, ice (crystal meth) or heroin, but prescription or over-the-counter medicines can also be abused, as can alcohol.

More than 3 million Australians use an illicit drug and about 1 million misuse a pharmaceutical drug every year. More than 40% of Australians over 14 have used an illicit drug in their lifetime, and illicit drugs are used by more than a quarter of people in their 20's each year. People from all walks of life take illicit drugs, and the type of drug they use can depend on their socioeconomic status including things like their cultural background, where they live and what their income is.

I encountered nutters in the blue mountains it can be a fucken nut case place. Scary Scarewee aaaaaa

1st YETI above my mission housing flat in Blackheath! A total selfish fuckwit that would bang on the floor above with what I suspect to be medicine balls every night at 1 – 3, then 5 am. My heart began to go awol, she yeti caused the previous tenant to have a heart attack. After a time with my partner responding violently – I ordered Bell to leave – I left.

Next up, was taking on old drunk Leigh's place in Wentworth Falls are we there yet, after he kicked it, with a granny flat downstairs (I thought I was safe). Alas Warwick Boatswain who lived in the granny flat later, a crim, parading around telling everybody he was a bank robber. Like Ned Kelly or Robbin Hood or Thunderbolt. As if that's cool. My partner falls for it as they gang up on me. Luckily Kym & Losa move in with me for a time, both suffering mild disability, and won't put up with this scoundrels behaviour. We find out he was a sex offender. After a time, we 3 split… slack help from the police meant no pathway to peace, I moved to Anketell forest Tento (Tenterfield) in peace and security> thanks Mr Steve Merta xx! Now I live with post trauma personality disorder/ I am octo polar and I have ABC DEFG HIJK LMNO P QRSTUV WXYZ I got all of it. I have joined the Oz demographic./

Risks associated with drugs abuse include physical and mental health problems, personal relationship issues, work and financial problems, drug addiction and drug overdose.

Around 1 in 20 Australians has an addiction or substance abuse problem. It can result in changes and long-term damage to the brain and other organs. Substance abuse is a major cause of mental illness.

A couple my friends have found success through this AA 12 step program, you may want to check it out...

1. We admitted that we were powerless over our addiction, that our lives had become unmanageable.

2. We came to believe that a Power greater than ourselves could restore us to sanity.

3. We made a decision to turn our will and our lives over to the care of God as we understood Him.

4. We made a searching and fearless moral inventory of ourselves.

5. We admitted to God, to ourselves, and to another human being the exact nature of our wrongs.

6. We were entirely ready to have God remove all these defects of character.

7. We humbly asked Him to remove our shortcomings.

8. We made a list of all persons we had harmed and became willing to make amends to them all.

9. We made direct amends to such people wherever possible, except when to do so would injure them or others.

10. We continued to take personal inventory and when we were wrong promptly admitted it.

11. We sought through prayer and meditation to improve our conscious contact with God as we understood Him, praying only for knowledge of His will for us and the power to carry that out.

12. Having had a spiritual awakening as a result of these steps, we tried to carry this message to addicts, and to practice these principles in all our affairs.

Morihei Ueshiba's quote fills my head with:

"the way of winning is not with violence".

I miss Hong Kong!

I also miss the use of my body! This is fucked! But I deal with it because I kung Fu Master.

"For the beginning guitarist, the first and most evident challenge is contorting one's fretting hand (left for a

I am Australian and bloody lucky for that.

HK introduced me to the practice and Kung Fu, allowed me many opportunities that I fulfilled. In addition, it allowed me to pursue and earn a living doing my music kung fu and I achieved nearly all that I wanted to do travel-wise with time spent in NYC, India, Banff, Oz. and SE Asia. Releasing independent music/CDS etc. It was a magical time. & a lot of hard work.

Now I'm home in my country, I am not a friggin' *Gawk-lo* or *Lao y, Gwai lo*. My people support me on many fronts and financially. As Daisaku Ikeda said "You can be happy anywhere!"

Guy Le Claire - Bandcamp

HEART ATTACK:

I succumb to a heart attack in Leura on Jan 18th, 2023 while cornered into yet another stressful situation.

This is very new to me, I cannot really comment on this area, but I can quote what's was written on my hospital discharge notice ... 'Estemi, myocardial infarction- high troppononin.

It was very freaky, I was screaming for help as I couldn't breath, the ambo's arrived feeding me oxygen they got me to emergency ward. Thank you Josh & Izabelle.

COVID March 2023:

As freaky as the scare was at the height of the covid pandemic, I sailed covid free, until recently in new home in QLD mum got it she lives upstairs, then I got it.

Others post pandemic suffered a fair bit, but I sailed pretty much asymptomatic no issues other than the tests proved positive, I'm always stuck inside anyway due to my disability so self isolation was no big deal. Later I got the flu, man that was painful.

Friday 24th June 2016 ado:

Aunty (a registered psychotherapist) says, *"this is probably as good as it gets"*. Doctor says *"You are doing remarkably well"*. Mum says *"Lazy little bugger"*.

2nd July 2016 6:45am - Adelaide SA

Today the nation votes to keep either, Malcolm Turnbull as Prime Minister and the Libs or for Bill Shorten ALP. Mind you, the smaller parties have gained some backing, since I lived away (since 1996 when Keating lost), so who knows? Malcolm has supported me with the Dole since I got back. I've applied for a pension and a number of other support systems. Still waiting on the ok of the pension, that comes so easy in HK, easier than the dole. The word *"eligible"* gets bandied around here non stop, I have learnt to pronounce it properly and respect it. Here in Oz to be eligible for a pension one needs to be examined by both private & government doctors – a permanent disability usually warrants a pension. Traditionally Dad and I are ALP voters.

Yesterday morning I had a Cortisone shot into my bad left shoulder, it made me feel a bit uneasy, especially last night with a racing heart, I feel ok now. Four days from now, I'm off to HK to visit LY, 30 + degrees, Li Yin and Yunnan noodle / Genki Sushi. I would have been back in Australia over 8 months and loved it. Definitely the care/medical is better and of course when you can speak my language :). Gotta sort out my storage and pension. Unfortunately money is a big player, without it we're stuffed. That little bit from HK has helped me out so much, used it for my return air ticket too plus get this book closer to the finishing line.

The Commodore needs a new radiator plus service, jeez! Might be looking at a thousand dollars for that, where da fuck to get the money? Jesus what a *sorlo*, having no life or health insurance as an expat, if you don't have any —GET IT!!!!!!!!!!!

Before my trip back up to Hong Kong, I say this where I've got to: International travel, I am able to get myself around somewhat independently, can hold conversations, walk albeit with a limp and some Spazzo, dress myself (which reminds me) ~

DON'T FORGET

Clothes labels for your upper torso – i.e: T-shirts, jumpers etc. Labels are located on the *inside Left* !

I'm a Lucky SOB!

But what I've experienced in my pursuit to recover has been a great journey, but it includes some painful realisations and myth Busting. I believe Western people reach for pinnacles in research and science, these breakthroughs are REAL and proven.

To recover, I currently wholly embrace a western scientific approach. If you should become sick, try to get the best of what we offer. Get home, don't dilly dally willy-wank away thinking some bullshit, get in with your prime recovery time frame. I believe in the truth of science. I have also become a believer in non-violence, so my KUNG FU is yet changing again, from Chinese Martial Arts and Kung Fu, which stems from *violence* to *non-violence and passivity.*

I feel and am blessed to be a citizen of Australia! You were right Gary Seib, better get back to Oz for some better care. Right on! Bro! From Surfer/Skier to Muso to Kung Fu to stroke survivor, its been a trip!

Nam Myo Ho Renge Kyo.

Adelaide Winter Australia xXX

----

a few memories...

FB Indonesia 1979

...November: Mum and I have landed in Djakarta, and somehow we get to Borobudur, we are then offered a ride to Surabaya and Solo that's all I can remember about Java '79... in 2015 I have a marvellous trip with Bellisa (her birthplace), training through Java to Bandung & onto Jakarta. It is magnificent.

FB 1998

...Talking of my wonder and respect of the United States of America. The United Kingdom always intrigued me, after all it is the United Kingdom, full of many kung fu stories. It was a lovely morning when Sylvia and I boarded The Flying Scotsman from London to Edinburgh. Gliding from the southern point heading north straight to Scotland, taking in beautiful British scenery with farmland so green it was hard to fathom the intense desire pursued to conquer other lands and remain there. Arriving in Edinburgh walking up the main road to secure our hotel, we then at my urging took a walk that first night to the lower area, below the precipice, went into a club focused on "Acid Jazz" and stayed a while. I later found out, that it was top Hong Kong *DJ Kulu's* crib, who I would work with down the track at wild DJ spins with live musoz gigs and parties... in HK...

I mull over the different languages of frustrated expression cursing for a while... *"motherfucker!"* *"Chinga tu madre"* (Mexico), *"diu lei lo mo"* (HK), *"ta ma de"* (China) and wonder how the sentence became so popular?

Bellisa! SEP We are best mates, we have fun – laugh, cajole, explore, feel very comfortable together. She is to quote Gap band 'you blow my mind, im so alive! Outstanding! Girl you knock me out, makes, me want to shout'. Amazingly we both love Black music, Bell dances none stop. Getting ready to die, since we are headed that way, both had our lives,. is sad and confronting. Bellisa's history is something like this, a Bandung girl, growing up middle class (with Citroens & Jeeps), her successful central Javanese father, Mr Gunadhi ruled with an iron thumb he dug Muhammad Ali, whilst her Dutch mother Francisca chilled amongst the 5 siblings – Monty, Christian, Patricia & Jessie. Today all is good but there are some squiblings. Bell escaped to Bali after a rough patch in 1983, there she ran into Australians Sandy & Gary. Gary & Bell hit it off big time. After much toing & froing they married here in Oz planning a house & family in which they succeeded, I met them as Gaz & I were in the Tribe. A strong friendship ensured, upon my arrival back in the blue mountains & Gary in heaven, my inner desire to connect, care, extend friendship to Bell was established. Pretty much since we have been inseperable. She entertains me with many amazing stories of her youth in Indo. We went there. post stroke btw:)

The Bell/guy roadtrip: 2017

Katoomba, Blackheath, Oberon, Goulburn, Canberra, Yass, Gundagai 'dog on tucker box', Wagga, Hay Plains, Balranald, Tail End, fill up /50 litres LPG about 40 bucks. Adelaide, Mums, Nomads Hutt st., Melbourne, Hume Highway, tucker box again, Penrith, Katoomba. The Commodore whizzed along real nice! VX.

Being alive is a gift, having an open mind and wishing to explore outside your box.. Get to it minus AI crap. Keep it Natural! Be aware of Mother Earth. Kiss her xxx.

The robots will take over!

Bell and I meandered around Wentworth Falls the other day and I decided to head for Tableland Rd, where Walter used to live and some photos of my son Julien and I were taken years ago. As we glided down the bitumen road we noticed skid marks and wheelies, plus a sign saying *Queen Vic Hospital*. As the tar ended a dirt road began, a huge thud in the commodore took place, we meandered along this dirt road for half an hour until I pulled over to check the GPS. There was no way we were going to get to the end of this road so I did a U-Turn and we headed back stopping at an open space eerie green area, noticing some buildings, the eerie vibe descended, I also noticed the back wheels very low on air., as I got out to do some kung fu. Driving on slowly we saw more buildings, all fenced in with 'ASBESTOS' signs stuck to them, pulling over left next to a huge tree we, took photos of this eerie vibe /place next to the now closed hospital (the internet has claimed it to be the spookiest place in Australia). Back where the thud happened and back on tar, I realised I had a flat tyre, I got the car to the highway and couldn't go on. The tyre was shot and unfortunately the rim cracked, good ole NRMA came to the rescue by way of the RAA. Since the road trip, our beloved Commodore seems to be falling apart, wheels/tyres, Amanda to the rescue $100 for 4 wheels. Stabiliser, fuel pump, air filter *(boom!!!)* and something is leaking. Unpleasant and Dangerous, **please avoid dusk driving!**

Back to our ado depature... we speed down the super freeway past Hahndorf (a place Bell loved) we hit Tailem Bend again, IGA, we're both thinking the Hay Plains "no way", so I don't turn off the Newell Hwy to go that way. Next thing *Melbourne* is only 300 ks away, so we reach the Grampians by dusk and Maccas free internet to book a room at Bell City in Melbourne, check in around 9pm and crash out big time.

MELBOURNE

Up earlyish, starting with a breakfast in Fitzroy, Melbz coffee & a foccacia .It is rather surreal sitting on Brunswick St. Melbourne is clearly a massive urban centre/city, it reminds me of NYC & Sydney. We end up in KFC Footscray, and I show Bell the apartment I bought with the ex-wife Sylvia, who Bell thinks is her "best friend". Signed all my property rights to her upon divorce in exchange for kids education fees to be covered by her. Achieved. I adore Melbourne such a magical city, that can compare to the best of them. Peak hour traffic to get back to Bell City apartment, we sleep, check out at 10am next morning and hit the road for Katoomba. The Hume Highway is totes different to when I was in bands, smooth double lanes each way allows the Commodore to sail, we get back to the dog on dee tucker box and it's press the pedal for our Blue Mountains turn off behind a Tesla doing 140 km/h for a while. Impatiently we exit on the first Penrith turnoff sign - mistake - and I'm stuck on the dumb Northern Road. Reaching the M4 and Blaxland I drive the car into the back of Merriwa St, 100 buckee dump to find Amanda, Iggy, Annie and Chris. We hug... Bellisa and I had made it! Darn what *KUNG FU IS THAT!* Our Kung Fu, not to mention the car's Kung Fu! Fuckin' carved it up, engine purred all the way. Now the car is falling apart, ha ha ha!

Time for me to drive Mum around South East Queensland. Katoomba temperature is on the cold/damp side, so I may go up north to get to warmer climates and the ocean. When I got out of hospital in HK, the first thing I did was hit St Stephens beach, bloody nice to swim (HK physio dude said I would sink, never did). It was in the salt water there that I could do double hands cloud hands *Chan Si Gong* again, whereas it had evaded me before. I have heard the ocean is the best doctor.

I am sitting in Katoomba Library with a stunning view vista out over the Jamison Valley and mountains. Mum has had issues with her property, and the buyer is pushing hard to shave more, $1,000's off the price. In two weeks I will pick up mum at Sydney airport, and haul her off to sunny climates and to view properties up north.

The Commodore (my car) performed exceptionally on our road trip, however, upon return she started to fall apart, air box blown, fuel pump, not to mention the tyre/wheel extravaganza on Tableland Rd. All up, $1000 bucks out of pocket. Sold my 2 guitars and FX box to cover it. Just have "REDDY" left, the 8 String electric Li Yin bought me, and a crappy amp. Oh yeah, sold my Fender Blues Amp, nice amp too.

Bell and I had been studying Boxing, watched Jack Johnson doco, and Joe Louis, all fascinating and can't wait to read Joe Louis book on boxing, I ordered nearly all the books in the Bruce Lee library. Since the road trip, I have come to realise that *driving* is a Kung Fu. And every single profession that you ever did or encountered as a devotee with passion is kung fu, good on youz. I particularly admire, well everyone, Motor Mechanics! Nurses! Farmers, the Lifesavers! and the Police.

Ashley from Garage 263 in Blackheath is another good mechanic like Michael from Quandt Motors in Adelaide. Ashley has the knowhow and flair of a kung fu man who really knows his cars. I asked his assistant "how do you guys know so much? Do you study, take courses or what? " He answered "Mate, been doing this for 38 years". That's what has consistently been blowing me out about being back in Australia, the folks find ways to fix things. Everything is fixable, unlike HKG where it gets chucked out "buy a new one". The more I stay away from HK, the more I do not miss it at all, I even despise it to some degree. It gave me much, then it just robbed me of everything. Fucking place! Having read Yvon Chouinard's book about his Patagonia Co. makes me realise how dumb HK is, really no awareness in a process of evolution or life principles, just *fast, fast! Money, Money...La!!* So unaware and ignorant.

Unfortunately I can now see it in my own kids (who were brought up there). How come I stayed on and on in HK? Ego/selfishness? Most of the top Aussie musos I sponsored to HK didn't have any desire to stay there and were pleased to get home.

I lived in fear of failure re Oz, I remembered the financially lean times back home, and willed myself to thinking how much of a big shot wanker I had become, with extra luggage emanating from Dad, about the bad side of Oz and the brilliance of a distant land. I was probably unfortunately deluded. But I did like very much Chinese culture and ways and women.

Here's something from Ravi Shankar's book "Raga Mala"... ..."To hear good jazz, I mostly had to go to jazz joints in the big cities like New York, San Francisco and Los Angeles. At these venues, even as all these brilliant musicians were playing, people would be drinking, smoking, eating and talking. Once in a while when a musician played an exciting solo, the audience turned their attention to him and showed their appreciation by clapping with real gusto. It was no wonder these jazz musicians bombed themselves with drugs and alcohol "numbing the senses." - this was pretty much the scenario in hk.

Once, A-Song said to me *"you know Guy, in the hierarchy of Chinese society, musicians sit at the bottom, below dancers and prostitutes"*.

Mum is super pleased to be selling her house in Ado, a down payment has been made and I will pick her up at Sydney airport to drive up to Hervey Bay. Perhaps that's where this book ends? I am constantly **flashing back**, any little thing gives me a **FB**. I also see designs and pictures in everything I look at: Clouds, Trees all produce *faces, figures,* all kinds of things, patterns more so than pre stroke, it can be quite entertaining at times. Sometimes I feel like

I'm going MAD. Bell just scored a job at Avalon restaurant, Katoomba, she is a smart girl.

May 16th, 2023

I now live in on Russell Island. QLD renting Mums cabin, A totally bent 'life with Bell meant I had to leave my beloved Bell & mountains.

.Mum to the rescue! However I migrate back to my favourite place in dee vorld BLUE MOUNTAINS.

Saturday 5th Aug 2017 kat

Just dropped Bell off to work. And I wonder if I'll ever get back to work, I would love to earn some extra dosh, to afford a few things. Inside the library, the winds outside are making a racket. The Commodore V6 just powers through nothing rattles it, I borrow car mags and admire the "muscle cars" that are now no longer made here (the government ought to have implemented an immigration policy, *Migrate to Australia buy Australian - 1st car*) that would have saved our cars, anyway as a continual dreamer, I wonder if my kung fu were cars and western science, would I have fared better? Well now it's pretty much those things.

FB Australia Singapore Paris

...Dad and I boarded UTA airlines DC-10 in Sydney bound for Paris via Singapore. We land in SQ and hop off for a re-fuel, hopped back on went hurtling down the runway when there was a loud bang, Dad at window seat said he could see an engine on fire, the pilot thrashed to a halt. We found ourselves at the Meridian hotel for the next three nights and both experienced our first taste of life outside Australia. It was Alien-nating yet we were fascinated. Dad helped the rickshaw driver push the thing up the road much to his disagreement. Finally we hopped on another DC10 coming from New Caledonia, with their football team onboard, a steward dressed as a stewardess came rollicking down the aisle with a trolley shouting *"Bon Bon... Bon Bon"* (sweets) in a high pitched female voice, everyone began laughing. Landing for a fuel stop in Abu Dhabi, dawn was surreal. Then onto Athens, a DC10 had gone down recently so I think we were all a bit nervous, especially after the SQ happening. Approaching Charles De Gaulle Airport into Paris, the plane banked severely and everyone screamed. Upon touchdown the whole plane applauded with shouts of "Bravo!!" Dad and I hopped in a taxi to our hotel on the Left Bank...

Letter to Li Yin my Chinese girlfriend...

Dear Li Yin,

Just a short note to express my gratitude, of your loving support for me during those two years, after I was discharged from hospital, you may never know how appreciative I am for all that you did, as an in- patient as well as an out-patient. However, as the evidence of our age difference became a heavy issue, especially with our families, I believe my decision to return to Australia was a good one.

You always told me to let you know if I "fell in love with someone else down here". That happened and I told you, Apologies for the hurtful way in which it was conveyed. You will always remain in my heart and soul. But sometimes we need to let go. I wish you all the very best and happiness and health for you.

Love Guy xxx

----

more memories...

FB May 1976...

Just after my 16th birthday I hopped on Canadian Pacific Airlines bound for Montreal where Mum was living with Eddy. The flight via Auckland, Fiji, Honolulu and Vancouver was on an old 707, it took about 40 hours and I was rat shit upon arrival to Mum, Pat and Howie Cohen. Waking up in Châteauguay (Montreal suburb where Mum and Eddy lived) the next morning, to a beautiful clear blue but crisply cool morning, all the neighbours were gardening topless, the place was so green! What followed I believe were bouts of jealousy as Mum placed lots of attention on her beautiful Prince/boy...

Mum and Eddy had planned to buy a van we could all live in and drive around South America. Eddy was a Chinese/Australian who was born in Shanghai, raised in hkg, then sent to Australia to finish his education, graduating with honours from UNSW in Architecture - he was to some degree my "Step-Dad". The Sth America trip wasn't happening, due to Eddy's *umming* and *ahhing* agitating Mum immensely, she would push Eddy's buttons, and big arguments would follow, I got kicked out and ended up living with one of mum's spunky friends (that I wanted to fuck) downtown.

FB: 1977…Wandering around Frida Kahlo and Diego Riveras house in Mexico City with Mum, first impressions back in Mexico after 20 years were not as mind fucking as China…

FB: Guangzhou, China …Dale Barlow and I are wandering around Guangzhou, Qingping St. and market, every conceivable animal is on display for consumption, with dark silhouetted men in side alleys smoking opium pipes. Returning a decade later to find silly touristy malls with shop sales people clapping to gain attention fake facade… An experience in Qingping market makes one realize that it's no wonder *SARS* evolved from Civet cats and uncommon animals in southern China…

Thich Nhat Kahn, the Venerable Vietnamese Buddhist Master has quoted that…*"we all should seek our own Clans religion, one doesn't need to be Buddhist to be a good person"* etc.

Pang Sifu has added this to his website:

Master Guy Le Claire

Sifu Guy Le Claire is a humble person and he finished his Head Coach Training course with Pang Sifu here in Hong Kong. He is living in the Blue Mountains, NSW Australia. He is approved in teaching the King 12 Moves for promoting health benefits in different aspects according to human biology, and the fa jin mysterious power in an interesting and safe way by modern physics of momentum law.

Master Guy has a very keen interest in Chinese culture and is a very famous musician in profession both here in Hong Kong and Australia. He lived in China for three years to learn Chinese kung fu and finally came to Pang Sifu, learning mysterious fa jin power by means of modern scientific ways. Master Pang is the founder of modern scientific Tai Chi. He wrote two books about the scientific fa jin theory and repeated the fa jin demonstrations of ten world grand masters in the DVD attached since 2012. He also did a 12 episode tv program in 2016 and reveals the application of the worlds most advance skills for tai chi power. At the same time, Guy joined the First World Champion Kung Fu Marble Power and won a Gold Prize Award, a game for training and to test internal kung fu in a safe and interactive way by internal delivery of body weight, developed by Pang Sifu.

Guy understood the power described in many kung fu frictions after following master Pang and is enlightened in mind about real kung fu. He believes this modern physics King Tai Chi is readily spreading to western developed countries based on its innate bio-physics nature.

(For Australia Class details, please contact Sifu Guy or through hk-williampang@gmail.com)

My concept of reality is altering...ive discovered as a stroker my brain & perception is different. Like I might be going mad!

Remember ~ We **all** have **KUNG FU**.

Be it

Farmers, Farming, Engineers, Car/Truck Drivers, Mechanics, Tradesmen, Musicians, Doctors, Nurses, Allied Health Professions, Artists, Public Servants, Inventors, Swimmers, Footballers, Cricketers, Surfing, The Gym, Carers, Caregivers, Hospitality, Teaching, Transport Workers, Dancers, Ballet, Painting, Painters, Skiing, Skiers, Cycling, Chefs, Cooking, Climbing, Scientists, Writers, Ambos, Emergency Volunteers, Firemen, Paramedics, Australian Defence Force, Police etc ~

Thankyou Heroes!

My take on it is Exercise **EXERCISE YOUR BRAIN, EXERCISE YOUR BODY**

What it boils down to is a **KUNG FU** is a lifestyle and attitude, all encompassing, all embracing, A Passion, Addictive, Unending.

We get into it, We are it and it is Us! **DO IT!!!!**

Do Everything You Can To Overcome ~ Please Don't Hurt Any Living Thing ~ Be Aware.

Awareness is very good.

Atoms: An atom itself is made up of three tiny kinds of particles called subatomic particle

Proton: is a particle with a positive charge that is in the nucleus of an atom

Synapses: In the nervous system, a synapse is a structure that permits a neuron (or nerve cell) to send and/or pass an electrical or chemical signal to another neuron.

Neurons: are electrically excitable cells that receive, process and transmit information through electrical and chemical means. The specialised synapses transmit signals between the neurons. There are approximately 100 billion neurons-nerve cells in the brain. *Stroke* typically kills about 2 billion.

Physics: literally *"knowledge of nature"*, it is the natural science that involves the study of matter and its motion and behaviour through space and time, along with related concepts such as en- ergy and force.

Stroke: brain injury

Neuroplasticity: the ability for the brain to rewire to the will of its owner.

Cognitive:

1. Of or relating to cognition; concerned with the act or process of knowing, perceiving, etc. Cognitive development: Cognitive Functioning.

2. Of or relating to the mental processes of perception, memory, judgment, and reasoning, as contrasted with emotional and volitional processes.

Semantic: relating to meaning in language or logic

Nei/ Ni Gong: internal skill, usually attributed to Chinese martial arts as soft or internal, as opposed to Wei/Hei Gong = out, Nei = in, - with philosophical foundations in Taoism

Dao Yin: Also Tao yin or Taoist *Neigong* is a series of body and mind unity exercises practiced by Taoists to cultivate Jing (essence). One of many Qi Gong.

Cell: The cell (from Latin *cella*, meaning "small room") is the basic structural, functional, and biological unit of all known living organ- isms. A cell is the smallest unit of life that can replicate independently, and cells are often called the "building blocks of life". The study of cells is called cell biology. Cells consist of cytoplasm enclosed within a membrane that con- tains many biomolecules such as proteins and nucleic acids.

Ego: A person's sense of self-esteem or importance.

Taoism or Daoism: A religious/philosophical tradition of Chinese origin that emphasises living in harmony with the Dao (Way/Law of all things in the universe).

A neuron with myelinated axons can conduct the impulse at a faster speed since the myelin sheath acts as the insulator that helps to propagate the electrical signal faster. A majority of the neurons in the central and peripheral nervous system are myelinated since they require fast conduction speeds.

Due to presence of Myelin sheath, myelinated nerves do not lose the impulse during conduction whereas Unmyelinated nerve fibres can lose the nerve impulse during conduction. The nerve fibres with long axons are Myelinated whereas the short axon nerve fibres are Unmyelinated.

Qi is an electric current in the body.

Kriya Yoga excerpt from Paramahansa Yogananda

"Babaji's mission in India has been to assist prophets in carrying out their special dispensations. His chief disciple was Lahiri Mahasaya, revivalist of the lost Kriya art. The science of Kriya Yoga became widely known in modern India through the instrumentality of Lahiri Mahasaya, my guru's guru. The Sanskrit root of kriya is Kri, meaning to do, to act and react; the same root is found in the word karma, the natural principle of cause and effect. Kriya Yoga is thus "union (yoga) with the Infinite through a certain action or rite". A yogi

who follows its technique is gradually freed from karma or the universal chain of causation.

Kria Yoga is a simple, psychophysiological method by which the human blood is decarbonised and recharged with oxygen. The atoms of this extra oxygen are transmuted into life current to rejuvenate the brain and spinal centres. By stopping the accumulation of venous blood, the yogi is able to lessen or prevent decay in tissues; the advanced yogi transmutes his cells into pure energy. Elijah, Jesus, Kabir and other prophets were past masters in the use of Kriya or a similar technique, by which they caused their bodies to dematerialise at will."

Kriya is an ancient science. Excerpt from Chapter 26 Yogananda's bio.

...and to continue..."God first created the earth as an idea. Then he quickened it; energy atoms came into being. He coordinated the atoms into this solid sphere. All its molecules are held together by the will of God. When He withdraws His will, the earth again will disintegrate into energy. Energy will dissolve into consciousness; the earth-idea will disappear from objectivity."

Could it be that myself and many others have confused *Qi* for *Atoms*? If previously my hypotheticals of *Qi Chi* were actually atomic, it may not be *Maya* - illusory. It's all fascinating stuff, and there is no doubt in my head that it all originated in North Africa (Egypt, Algeria, Sudan, Saudi Arabia), Himalayas/ Nepal and the dry Central Asia. Then developed in India & Persia.

India is really at the centre of things. It ought to be called "ZHONG GUO"!!! Ay A-Cha?

2020

I'm out and about in Blackheath. Funnily enough, bump into Stephen who asks me why are Chinese Mainlanders and HKers so preoccupied with money? I couldn't answer him, so I just googled it, it only talked about how the physical Chinese money (coins) had holes in it. Ha Ha Haaaaaaaaaaaa. ...I saw a girl crossing the road the other day with some tattoos on her lower legs, the most interesting observation was that she had long thin lines tattooed on her back legs, like u could unzip them. Left /Right. This is exactly how I feel with an invisible line separating my left from my right. Starting at my nose and cleft it goes all the way down to my anus crack and has me numb & tingly on the left with normal sensation on the right. Luckily my cock feels normal as I think so do my left and right balls.

This book may never end... are we there yet? Peter G Levine in his book *Stronger after Stroke* states that the *"extremities like hands are usually last to recover"* are you there yet?

WOW! The whole country, indeed the whole planet is going into "Lockdown" due to the Corona Virus COVID-19, it is a living, terrifying nightmare. I may have seen SARS in HK and its destructive path but I was able to take off for YS. Mum wants me to move back to Adelaide. State borders are shut and this virus is everywhere and arresting all, there's no escaping or running away this time! *DIU*

Stuart Alve Olsen is an interesting cat producing all manner of books on Taijiquan etc, I better go to bed now as I have my free Tai Ji session gift to community to give in 7 hours up at the square across the road.

Goodnight

Lets look at Hong Kong

The unforgivable fact that domestic helpers, mainly from the Philippines and Indonesia do not attain any PR Residency, even after 7 years residency, exhibits an underlying racist law still carried on today. The Brits arrived in this part of southern China, and set up base upstream of the Pearl River in Guangzhou. It was illegal for foreigners to learn Chinese (another racial slur), horribly the Brits started trading opium drug as legal tender for Chinese goods. This created mayhem just like the foreign businessmen expats in HK that got addicted to cheap 'ice' replacing expensive coke habits due to the Asian Tiger financial crisis period and began failing their families and jobs... after the opium wars, the territory of Hong Kong including the New Territories and Kowloon were ceded to the UK for 100 years to 1997. I was there at the handover, ensconced with my band in the Conrad Hotel in Pacific Place (a Swire group initiative) overlooking the ceremony down at the Convention Centre. By a jostling of western and eastern ways, HK worked like a machine and was able to survive and become prosperous. Over the decades, both the Brits and Chinese learnt from each others cultures and ways, each believing their race superior to the other. The Chinese always valuing education, sent their children to Britain to learn and the foreigners made lots of money. Like a marriage they had their ups and downs, and resentments. As the UK previously was the leader in the world in might, power and technology, it was a magnet for megalomaniacs. As China radicalised in 1949 just 70 miles away, people fled in fear of the new mainland regime to HK to escape the political turmoil going on in the "Motherland". The population exploded and the Brits with their engineering feats turned HK into an engineering marvel with schools and hospitals provided and compulsory (Governor MacLehose is respected).[SEP] Just about every HK Chinese I ever met was either A: born in *China* or B: parents are from *China*. That's why I never understood the 2014 "Occupy Movement". It later spurned resentment if not hatred towards Mainland Chinese people belittling them, in addition to the mainland government. All HK Chinese are mainland derived. It was also run by a bunch of kids fresh out of high school and in HK University, with no policies. A good example of spoilt little HK fuckers. There is an uneasy queasiness about hkers, on the racial front a competitive/ face value/ identity crisis verging on being dangerous, a pseudoness of artificial-dom, and a totes focus on money, stunting any kind of human growth (unfortunately I can say I've read HK's two famous son's biographies Bruce Lee and Jackie Chan, their stunted humanity is selfish and childishly annoying). As the UK's power waned and the USA's increased, it was more fashionable to send the kids to the US for education. So went our little *Brucee* (it helped that he was born in San Fransisco because his mum was pregnant with him while dad played Chinatown). Since then to now, we have many HK celebrities who grew up in the US and went back to HK with their skills and black vibe African/American culture of greetings, dance, music and jive. Lee was the first, Donnie Yen, Daniel Wu, Khalil Fong are *ABC* and the list goes on. Young Asian kids, who think they are fashionable like to copy the Black American urban youth culture. It is trendy.

ABC: Can now mean in addition to American born Chinese, Australian born Chinese, like my kids. Speaking of which, my son is at this moment sitting on a Qantas flight from Syd to HK. Just like I used to many times before...As much as I'd like him to stay in Oz along with all my reasons and theories, I secretly understand why he wants to go back there, just like HK had a gravitational pull for me and Bruce Lee. He wasn't de only one. I be too busy looking good / been practicing huh!?

Random Blabbering

Wan Chai, Hong Kong

Such a fucken funny weird place, I'm not surprised it turns up again in this book. A district sandwiched between Central and Causeway Bay, Wanchai has many pubs, bars, restaurants and girlie bars. Jaffe Rd runs parallel with Lockhart road, nearby on reclaimed land lies the Grand Hyatt Hotel, the immigration and tax revenue towers. The area is frequented by ex-pats who like to drink, look at and pick up chics, mostly whores. The film the *World of Suzie Wong* is set here. Every Sunday the domestic helpers (*helpers holiday* is Sunday) flock there to find a catch and hang. Domestic Helpers are 99 per cent women and originate from nearby Philippines and Indonesia, probably from a little village, who cater to local and ex-pat hong konger's families as the husband and wife are too busy working, or fucking around. They get paid hk$2,500 a month to do basically -everything and get temp work visas and have every Sunday off. The pretty ones hang for a catch, an ex-pat or Chinese bloke who will "sponsor" them so they have an easier life and all they have to do is FUCK. It works both ways as old geezers hang onto their beer and young sweetheart. I walk around ready to *chuckup.*

I myself was caught by the fishing line and sponsored one lady. We had a good time until the whole thing backfired. It was a *Roman's* dream that went terribly sour! So they are all down there in Wan Chai on Sundays. I was staying with my mate, Mr Allen Youngblood there when I came back from Adelaide, and like a lot of ex-pats we'd be down at one of the bars for afternoon drinks. At the *Jungle Bar* in comes Pierre Ingrassia, a massive dangerous hulk of a guy who owns *The One* martial arts club in Central. He starts ordering shots of tequila and frequently runs to the dunny for a line of coke waving around trying to tell us about his big deal bringing MMA to Macau - now a gambling/Casino Mecca rivaling Las Vegas, a little *Filipina* rocks up and he takes her to the dunny for a blow job, comes back with a smile and carries on, then disappears. This routine was repeated each time Allen and I go back (which was everyday). Then not too long after we find out the ole Pierre was found dead in a Love Hotel. In his obnoxiousness, he had a good spot/heart.

I had met him ages ago and he knew that I loved kung fu. We shared something. It was sad news to hear of his demise.

I first landed in HK in 1979 (at the ole Kai Tak Airport) with Mum who was based there, we lived in Yung Shue Wan, Lamma Island, it was idyllic. I made Chinese friends - we constantly debated over which was better Wing Chun or Pak Mei (white eyebrow kung fu), I also made great friends with Karl Derrick and Dale Wilson (who spoke fluent Chinese and looked like Jesus), I just cruised for a while, then I began Wing Tsun Kuen with Sifu Po Kin Wah in Mongkok. A chance to head over to Boston to study at Berklee College of Music had me on my way, then onto London and Paris where Dad was living. I missed my then girlfriend Sylvia, whom I had met on a long weekend away with Dale, Mum and the Lamma Baha'I Faith in Shenzhen in 1979. Back then it was a little village with a MacDonalds, absolutely nothing like it is today. Sylvia liked Dale, I liked Sylvia, the little girl from Sham Shui Po. I personally adored the vibe of Asian women, romantic, cute the opposite of Aussie aggressive assertive women. Call me a wimp! A decade later she was pregnant with our son Julien so I promptly married her in Sydney on the 19th August 1990. A year later Nastassja our daughter was born in Katoomba Anzac hospital.

Living on Lamma there were often fights between drunken expats (usually a Brit) and one of the village boys, both were loud and proud, but the real fact is that one couldn't survive without the other...Hong Kong was simpler in the 70's and 80's, it was a time bubble. The locals were terrified of the impending handover and migrated to Canada, Australia, UK and USA. There, the ABC and CBC's were born and educated. Finding their way back to HK -one country 2 systems - they had developed skills, much like an Aussie migrant going back to their birthplace to find success, except HK has the money and pathways to media stardom. Let's look at Donnie Yen born in Guangzhou. He grew up in Boston where his mum was an established *Nei Jia* martial artist. The young Don followed his mothers' skills a broadminded American citizen, he also pursued most martial art styles and had the opportunity & time to think and assimilate and develop his way. He put the hard work in with practice, upon his arrival in HK, he gravitated towards modeling, moving pictures, the young Donnie did his first movie at age 21, he now is a kung fu superstar. Most of HK's current actors have similar paths, two exceptions today are Jet Li (mainland) & Jackie Chan (local bred/raised), Jackie went through the legendary HK China Drama School at Peking Opera Academy in HK, where *The Seven Little Fortunes* were produced. JC along with Sammo Hung Kam Bo, Yuen Biao, Yuen Wah - totes HK raised and bred. I asked Jackie which style he likes most? His reply was along the lines that all styles of kung fu share the same traits, he doesn't prefer one over the other just like Chinese Kung Fu.

In hindsight about HK, the strange phenomena of being for example: a Christian and believing in God, yet still adhering to old traditional ritualistic rites, having an altar with the images and statues of the god of war and justice and one of wisdom, one for prosperity, used to do my head in! It seems so 'Double-Standard'. Like lets do both for the benefits. Sylvia is and has been a Christian since her teens. When her father, *Gung Gung* passed on, it was a Chinese funeral. Burning all manner of things for the afterlife and all dressed in white like the Klu Klux Klan, when we left you never look back.

With the recent passing of her mum *Po Po*, who wasn't of any particular denomination leaning more to traditional, everyone wore black and it was a Christian funeral service. It's like the movie *The Foot Fist Way* where the jerk main character's wife keeps fucking whoever's better than her husband that comes along. The HK custom has to be taken as coming from peasant backgrounds, folk customs and animism, rituals that have existed as a backbone in their ways and culture. So no need to intellectualise it and get all hung up boy! Just accept it, as no doubt other acceptable religious beliefs became part of society – overlapping. Lap dancing.

Back in HK, some of the common phrases in Canto are pretty harsh like *"diu lei lo mo chau hai"* (fuck your mothers smelly cunt) or *"ham sup lo"* literally translates to *salty wet person* (dirty old man). I believe this emanated from the fact that the Tanka women who lived on boats on the sea were the only ones that would fuck foreigners, as Chinese women couldn't bear to fuck them as it was shameful. Sea women were wet and salty and a guy that fucked them must therefore be wet and salty *ham sup lo*.

When I got settled back in HK, after 3 years in China, and ducking around I managed to create a lucrative teaching business in Clearwater Bay, a beautiful place sandwiched between Sai Kung and Tseung Kwan O. I had a freestanding house in Mang Kung Uk village, and loved HK and was proud that I had made it alone for the last decade without ever going on a dole or whatnot.

The language problem is a big problem. Two jokes are that;

India benefitted from the English as they speak more eloquently than most native english speakers after the Brits left ... and

HK was the best Chinese take away ever! From the Brits, but their English is shite.

So many misunderstandings from language misinterpretations. The English shot themselves in their own foot by allowing the English translations of Cantonese to go ahead the way they did. It continually makes Gwailos' sound dumb when there is no structure, go figure. How do you say *"Tsimshat tsui"*? Well in local ...it's *"Sim sa jui"* or *"Mongkok"*? It's *"Wong gock"*. It is so wrong. The mainland got it right with developing the **Pin Yin** system, once learnt and understood, ain't no going wrong. My canto is real basic, I have learnt essential phrases, I know a lot of phrases and can say them something akin to a local, but cannot hold conversation.

Li Lian Jie – *"Jet Li"* born and bred in China joined the national Wu Shu team. Became a performer (the mainland preferred the performance kung fu - Wu Shu, it eradicated the martial/violent nature, probably to promote peace amongst it's people and create it as a national sport) the Chinese killed more Chinese than any other race (inc. the Japanese). Once a Chinese man said to me *"You are lucky you are not a Chinese"*! I met Li Lian Jie at the Chinese Youth League where I used to train with teacher Fong in the mid 80's in Sydney's Chinatown. He had just filmed "Shaolin Temple" and was yet to become super famous, he did have a higher air about him compared to his team-mates.

Jet Li visiting Chinese Youth League Sydney1986

I had played (most Chinese kung fu people say 'play' rather than train or study) Yau Gung Mun, Choy Lay Fut in Chinatown but settled with Fong in Long Fist Wu Shu at the Chinese youth league. He learnt all his forms from books he bought in a Chinese book store in Dixon St. Funnily enough I began buying heaps, but have lost nearly all my intimate belongings from moving so much, what I have left is a book Ba Duan Jin I gave Dad, I wonder what would have been if Dad had taken it up.

Guy and Tiger Chen at the *Man of Tai Chi* after party

Author with Keanu Reeves at the after party for the filming of the movie *Man of Tai Chi* 2013 HK.

Dad's character was quite old school Aussie, hippies were wankers, pot is out, beer and vino in. etc etc. Mum on the other hand is quite alternative, loves a drink, smokes heavily but begins everyday with either lemon water or apple cider vinegar, takes Vitamin supplements and eats well, prays to a Buddha statue, does daily meditations, in particular, a lying meditation combined with deep breathing exercises, she is totes amazing and I'll be attending her 80th birthday in Adelaide next week. Dad was fucked by the age of 59, both sides fucked left and right, eyes totes out of whack, peripherals fucked, speech fucked, totes fucked.

So Mum is amazing.but she can be a bitch!

"The Secrets of Bama"

used by permission of Ma Li Yin.

Located in the northwest part in Guangxi, Bama Yao Autonomous County is around 4 hours drive from Nanning City. Bama is so famous for its natural scenes and longevity of its residents, making me so curious and excited on our way there.

Upon arrival, what appeared in front of us just made us speech- less. The feeling reminds me of the poem of Drinking Wine(飲酒) by the ancient Chinese poet Tao Yuan Ming(陶淵明) - '*I built my house near where others live. Still there's no sound of wheels or voices. You'll ask me "How can that be?" When the mind is remote the place is distant.*'(結廬在人境,而無車馬喧。問君何能爾?心遠地自偏) The mountains in Bama are not that high, but seem to extend and stretch on forever. The bamboos in Bama are quite unique too, they are everywhere, but not like those elsewhere else in China, these Bamboos are tall but not remote, always giving us a humble posture. And the lake surrounded by the greens is quiet like a mirror, the fisherman that turns up in his little boat occasionally can make it even quieter and more secluded. Involved in this at- mosphere, everything seems to have slowed down a bit. Even the caterpillar on the wall looks cute while the sun sets.

By the Cifu Lake there ('Ci' means 'Give' - 'Fu' means 'Happiness'), I suddenly started doing some Taiji forms unconsciously. I did wonder where and how come Taiji just came from at that moment. As a Chinese, I guess maybe the flow with Qi and spirit of Taiji is in my blood, or it's merely because of the breeze of the winds among the beautiful mountains in the rain made it so special and natural that day. The beauty of Bama is so unusual but arbitrary, Like Laozis' philosophic ideas of 'square-edged but does not scrape; having corners but does not jab; spread out but does not encroach on others; shining but does not dazzle, and I wonder whether that's one of the reasons why the residents there have long lives.

People in Bama told me that there might be plenty of reasons for their longevity. Air, diet, water, location, magnetic fields of the earth etc. The food that impressed me the most there in Bama are the 'Oil Fish', together with the tofu and soup made with Huo Ma 火麻

seed or oil. People in Bama call the local fish 'Oil Fish' because the fish seeps oil (fat) and smells so good when its fried (and to be honest, these little fatty fish is quite tasty), also the locals call these fish the 'Ginseng underwater'. The other unique food that attracted me is the *Huo Ma (Hemp seed)* seed, which is a special treasure in Bama. Apparently, local people use this cold pressed oil or seed in their cookings frequently. Being called the 'Super Food', Huo Ma seed contains Omega 3 and 6 fatty acids, plenty of plant-based protein, vitamins A, E and D, plus many B vitamins – all important antioxidants that help eliminate free radicals in the body. No wonder the local people always say, "*Have Huo Ma (火麻) everyday and live to 98*" ('Huo Ma' and '98' rhyme so well in Chinese:).

I was so lucky in our journey to visit a local couple there in Bama, the Li family. Mr. Li Yun Sheng and his wife, both nearly 100 years old, can still see and hear clearly while talking fluently. To my surprise, they told me that there's no secret to living a long life. Throughout their whole lives, they always *'go to bed with the lamb, and rise with the lark'*. And at the age of nearly 100, they still keep the habit of going out to have a walk along the mountain path everyday. So I guess their way of living with the logic of *'Imitation of the Nature'* as the Taoism might be one of the other reasons for their longevity. Like in a fairytale, they live together happily ever after.

In Bama, all the sensations can be awoken and sharpen within one day, my eyes can see greener mountains and bamboos, my nose can smell fresher air, my mouth can taste the most original flavour of the natural food, my ears can recognise so many different kinds of birds and insects singing, the beauty of which is beyond description. And there's definitely no need to be too shocked if one day you find yourself all of a sudden become a poet or a painter, a singer or a dancer, or even a *Taiji* master. At least I won't be surprised at all, not at all.

By Ma Li Yin

some friends have died, which leaves me on the depressed side. Also with the looming move back to mums. I've asked Bellisa to marry me but she won't. How come I always pick women that won't marry me!!!? She has agreed to a companion ceremony, I am thrilled! Darn I love her.

If you get the chance to come here to Australia and if you are here, travel around this wonderful country, be open, polite and social, get into the fabric of the place. Australia does have it's problems, but on the whole it's a fairly easy going distinctive place.

Bell and I are able to chat about anything, and I can blabber!! But we dig each other's company so much. There is a deep love there.

Bruce determined to succeed and make money, fashionable Eurasialien Bruce did it!

"We are all one Family, under One Sky" - Bruce Lee

BROTHERS

I am an only child meaning no siblings, but I can state that I have two HK brothers and one Oz brother.

Mr. Flynn Adams - extraordinary bassist from USA, and **Mr. Robbin Harris** - drums, emerging potter together with Flynn we formed *Z-Men* in HK. *Z-men* maintained a residency at *Mes Amis,* Wanchai that lasted a good while. We eventually released a *Z-Men* CD sponsored by one of our fans. As people and musoz we bonded deeply. Sadly, Flynn passed on earlier this year 2019, both Robbin(Canada) and I (Oz) made it to his funeral in HK - our old home –for me courtesy of Sam & Olaf Vogee. Darn I miss them.U Don noodle.

And my one Aussie brother, the collaborator of this book **Mr. Chris Frazier** - muso/bassist.

Robbin Harris, Chris Frazier & Guy Le Claire at Peel Fresco in Hong Kong Jan 2012

Both Robbin and Chris are rare, lovely people. Indeed they both sent me computers as mine was on the brink, to help me continue writing this book. In addition, Robbin shared his area of expertise with the world during lockdown. Posting home workouts on you- tube that may have been beneficial to those in sedentary lifestyles. Robbin is willing and putting out positive vibes for all to see.

Chris is able to find solutions and ways of fixing almost everything. I am constantly in awe of this kung fu method of most Australians and with Chris in particular, he is a genius to me. Fuck I love 'em. U don noodle!

As mentioned, I have been fortunate as an only child to have in particular two brothers in this world - I first met Chris Frazier when we were at Neutral Bay Primary in 1971, we both completed our education there and then went on to Mosman High maintaining our friendship, then both continuing on into our respective musical careers. My very first band **"Los Tres"** was with drummer Simon Baderle and Chris on bass. We used to rehearse at Chris's house in Cremorne. A neighbour nearby heard us and booked the band for a gig the following weekend. We literally passed our gear over the side fence to set up. They had even built a stage for us. We were fed and paid $10 each, though the funny thing was, we only knew 3 tunes!!

Chris dad Jim passed away recently Jim sent me his book 'Through the Lens' a magical read and his accentuation of Awareness of our planet drill.

PLEASE BE AWARE OF OUR PLANET WE ARE KILLING HER!!!!!!!!!!!!!!!!!!!!!!!!

My other brother is Robbin Harris whom I met in HK circa 1998. Robbin, an American Canadian arrived in HK from Taipei where he was based at the time, desperately wanting to get back on drums and gig, he showed up at number of times at my HK gigs, strategically complimenting my playing, likening it somewhat to John Abercrombie (which sat well with me). When he decided to hang around HK, I began booking him for gigs, and thereafter our friendship and respect for each other blossomed.

FB 1977 ...It's a Friday after school, Chris and I have tee'd up to meet up at Spit Junction and catch a bus into the city to see a movie, I had dropped a trip after school. We meet up, hop on the bus and Chris begins one of his verbal diarrhoea spiels that I previously zoned out on, however this time as the trip kicks in, I am totes flabbergasted by what he has to say I'm so into it. Upon alighting at Wynyard I say *"let's go to Hyde Park before the movie"*, I want to show him the statue of Captain Cook, which when viewed at the right angle, looks like he's *got a huge erection*. We observe this, and it's all get- ting a bit too much for me so I run away and climb a tree hiding. Chris is yelling *"Guy, Guy"* but I won't come down. After a time he decides to leave, I remain in the tree...

FB ...Robbin is infatuated with his beautiful cock, and begins to frequently display his "penis puppetry". *Z-men* band (Robbin, Flynn, Guy) has a gig at *"Le Rideaux"*, HK. The night before, Robbin happened upon a *Hens Night* at *"Joyce is Not Here"* HK, and proceeds to jump up naked to give the girls a thrill. This time at *Le Rideaux*, we have played a good show, albeit not to many people. As I thank the audience and venue at the end, I ask Flynn and Robbin if they want to add or say something, Flynn declines, however Robbin jumps up centre stage with spotlight on, and asks the remaining punters if they have ever seen a "hamburger" or "caterpillar". He pulls his pants with undies down with his cock flopping around, while Flynn and I run behind the stage giggling....'cause we know what's gonna happen, after a few minutes the PA and lights all go off. Robbin did his thing! Awesome...

FB 1978 ...Rolf and I have dropped a trip and we are outside "The Royal Antler Hotel" trying to get in and see Midnight Oil. The bouncer won't let us in, so we go round the back where the roadies load in and plonk ourselves down, leaning against the sliding doors. The sound and energy emanating from inside is incredible. After some time I say let's try and get in, we walk round the front and walk right in. Peter Garrett is overwhelming, with his bald head in the spotlight, and spaz dance moves, Jim Moginie is a saint, with Mar- tin Rotsey prowling like a panther. It is totes overwhelming and good. Definitely a bunch of Aliens communing with God...

Forgotten Years by Midnight Oil - check it out dudes

My neighbour in Mang Kung Uk village, Mr. Chung (who is built like a brick-house) stated that as he had been a village boy all his life, he had seen alien spaceships numerous times. He adamantly believes it, I didn't venture to ask if he had actually met any of the aliens ... *"Proof of the pudding is in the eating"*

That HK alien spaceship took me away on 1st June 2014

FB ...In China, westerners are called *"Lao Wai"* out side people, not a cursive HK vibe of "lei hai Gwai Lo!". In Australia it is now unacceptable to use the terminology of my youth like *Boong, Wog, Dago, Spick* etc. In fact it is against the law. However in the USA we get labeled as Aliens, that suits me fine...

I can't remember if I told you that when I was admitted into the HK hospital suffering stroke, I woke up the next day in a stroke ward, and believed I had entered an Alien Spaceship the night before and was spewed out an Alien stroker, after I don't know how long, only Li Yin knows. I was transferred to a Re-Hab Hospital, another Alien Spaceship. So, I am an *AustrAlien* :} thx Louis Burdett.

Fucken nappies, told to shit in them, fuck! Where the fuck was I? The Re-hab Hospital Ward didn't change nappies in the middle of the night, we all squelched praying for a change. The change came as some vague sighting of daylight revealed itself. The fucking ward stunk! To this day I thank and acknowledge all nurses in this profession. Fucking amazing creatures!

https://youtu.be/pumtoPyAhF

We all have choices, I hope this little book has imbued some positive element to your path so far. Good luck!

'Yoga is the teacher of yoga; Yoga is to be understood through yoga. So live in yoga to realize yoga; Comprehend yoga through yoga; he who is free from distractions enjoys yoga through yoga.' BKS Iyengar.

"Jazz is the Teacher, Funk is the Preacher" James Blood Ulmer

stroker tales:

I am infatuated with this nail on my thumb, how it flicks back and forward giving a painful sensation, should I bite it off? But I don't. This is my day la...

Freddie Hubbard = Straight Life.... Well the Stroke Life continues la.... I've moved back to Katoomba, *I am psychic and telepathic.*

I used to eat my boogies especially at Neutral Bay Primary, along with Mullberrys that grew along the fence. I don't eat them anymore, but I love the feeling of picking my nose. Especially when I find a good chunky one.

18th Dec 2019 kat

Darn the bushfires around here have really gone off. This morning waking up I could smell it in my little bedsit, smoky outside...

Autumn was too damp for Tai Chi – damp Qi not good, winter was too cold, now summer is too smoky- advice is to stay indoors – I can't win with getting out to play Tai ji la!! Ran into Peter Kinch – one of our mountains hot guitarists and his wife the lovely effervescent Louise at the Sushi Bar in Coles, their friend lived in Japan for an extended time and wrote a book, they encouraged me to move ahead with this here. I've bit my thumb nail off, and now I cant spade out the boogers inside my nose, *ho ma faan a!*

The issue is now the nail has been bitten so low, that my forefinger continually feel it, it brings a little pain. But I like it, so now I can't stop feeling it, as the Divinyls said *"There's a fine line between Pleasure and Pain".*

I was so proud and grateful that bass man Steve Hunter and I formed Australian super-fusion group *Playdiem* with David Jones – drums and John

Foreman- keys, I was able to explore most of my musical concepts, with very fine players indeed!

FB

...Steve Hunter drives around in a Saab *turbo*, I am in a relatives Merc, I sight him as we drive around the old Quays of Darling Harbour heading to our *Playdiem* gig at the Harbourside Brasserie located on Sydney Harbour. I speed up so I can sit on his tail, beeping and flicking lights, as we round the last corner we seelots of people lined up outside the Brasserie waiting to get in, it is surreal that we are seeing this for *OUR* gig. Full House... I was fucken nervous that night! La.

What tremendous skill and agility these 3 musoz have, I am frequently over-awed on stage by the roar backing me up from the rhythm section, something I will never forget la!...

Darn I wanna get that boogie out!

Have you ever found yourself in a time frame? It's a freak game Can't find an exit door 'Cause you're tied to the floor Running round and around and round Till you become a bore

Can't diffuse the situation, so you creep into the corners of your mind Ohh I want to ....

(From "Slit", Part of my YS Songs project).

"Where the mind is without fear and the head is held high; Where knowledge is free; Where the world has not been broken up into fragments by narrow domestic walls; Where words come out from the depth of truth; Where tireless striving stretches it's arms toward perfection; Where the clear stream of reason has not lost it's way into the dreary desert sand of dead habit; Where the mind is led forwardly Thee into ever widening thought and action; Into that heaven freedom, my father, let my country awake!" Rabindranath Tagore.

Roses to the left, Roses to the right, Roses front and behind, Rose, Rose, Roses

Law of Motion/ Universal Gravitation: Science until before the Theory of Relativity was realized and quantified by Isaac Newton. "Prism separates white light into the colours of our visible spectrum" The Alchemist.

"If I have seen further, it is by standing on the shoulders of giants" Sir Isaac Newton.

In Newton's eyes, worshipping Christ as God was idolatry, to him the fundamental sin. Newton insisted that divine intervention would eventually be required to reform the system, due to the slow growth of instabilities.

1st August 2022:

Anketell Forest, Tenterfield 6 months spent on mates Steve Merta's sprawling New England wildlife sanctuary property escaping crim psycho Warwick Boatswain.

Steve invited me to live in his Kung Fu Cottage he built me. I spent 6 months up there until the magnetism of the blue mountains & Bellisa drew me back. I now live in Leura. I will forever be blue mountainised. Time spent somewhere then back again. Are we there yet?

With Steve we managed a band reunion in Qld with Will Scarlet, Dario Bortolin & leader – Bob Tehira = For Sale band- more in my kung fu music.

Most of us survived! (the pandemic) Although last month at 5am staring out of kung fu cottage I saw an alienspaceship glittering like a centipede in the frosty clear dark New England sky above. Put me in a right spin. Later found out it was Elon Musk's Space X satellites. *I thought I was gonna be picked up again, I went outside to confront it like a man.*

Road trip qld

Steve and I are taking a road trip to 1770 north of Bundaberg, to reunite with our bandleader Bob, we depart the anko property to head to Twin Towns to reunite with Will Scarlet & Dario Bortolin who is performing with the Baby Animals. We make it and unite, the Animals are special zone stuff. Leaving the next day to we hang with artist Geof, a few days there we make it finally to Bobs. Bob is in a zone all by himself, exclaiming that in the For Sale days I seemed to have lost my commitment to de band, I have nothing to say, but know I wanted to be in Miles band not a cover show band!

Qld seems too wealthy, and I don't dig it, sorry. The beaches are owned by dickheads, they're not public with access, the whole place reeks in Joh corruption. We drive through macadamia, sugar cane, papaya plantations but no local produce is for sale on the road or in local villages, even the coast is the same. No local seafood. Crap! It is all destined for large prices & international consumption, money, money, Money! To sponsor the great Australian dream of a boat, a caravan, a property with many rooms & aircon & heating, plus guns & the latest wanky toys. Wankers! I have developed a theory that everyone in qld is dead already, money inspires them to go out & work all day.

Are we there yet? Strewth!

We make it to Gladstone my fathers town. Steve goes for a haircut I head to the pub atop de knoll, where I think my grandpa was interred in the pub fridge. Zoe the barmaid is chatty & mentions the fridges are in the basements, along with reputed ghosts. I think I've found grandpa and see dads environs, which I like, I have a pacific ale in remembrance of em. cheers!

Visiting mum in Moreton Bay we are stoked to be back in anko after 3 weeks! After spending 1k on the 380 – timing belt, she purrs all the way. Made in Ado dat one with oz jap techno!

Finally I sucuumb to living in Qld and begin to enjoy it actually, more affordable with local people providing for local community, the fauna is different more like SE Asia. But there are no Asian babes! I exist between the island & Katoomba. But miss istriku always.

I think I now know & understand … Aussies worked all their lives, at the end of their work career they want a comfortable end of life, with good weather, facilities and affordability – the answer Qld!

Asian & other migrants plan on going back their homeland/birthplace, with their savings & a pension to live out their days back there, the shitholes cheap, family will take care dem. Everyfing cheap. Australia is a strange existence of Work, piss up, Sport.

With Music & the Arts at the bottom & Qld as a repository of old school Australia relishes in this cultural existence. The old school Aussies will die out and everything will be fucking boringly woke. FUCK!!!!!!!!!!

Deepwater NSW (near Anketell):

is that a man? No, its a woman:):):)

Living on the Land was a priceless experience I recommend it to everyone! KEEP IT REAL

2022 back in dee blue mountains and with beautiful Bellisa: Leura. What a fucking nightmare that turned out to be. 2023 but I'm back sorlo?

That HK alien spaceship took me away on 1st June 2014

"Where the mind is without fear and the head is held high; Where knowledge is free; Where the world has not been broken up into fragments by narrow domestic walls; Where words come out from the depth of truth; Where tireless striving stretches it's arms toward perfection; Where the clear stream of reason has not lost it's way into the dreary desert sand of dead habit; Where the mind is led forwardly Thee into ever widening thought and action; Into that heaven freedom, my father, let my country awake!" Rabindranath Tagore.

Roses to the left, Roses to the right, Roses front and behind, Rose, Rose, Roses

Law of Motion/ Universal Gravitation: Science until before the Theory of Relativity was realized and quantified by Isaac Newton. "Prism separates white light into the colours of our visible spectrum" The Alchemist.

"If I have seen further, it is by standing on the shoulders of giants" Sir Isaac Newton.

REMEMBER YOUR KUNG FU "BECAUSE WE ALL HAVE IT!"

And also, tee-shirts or pants, most clothes have a label on the inside left, this will enable you to dress appropriately, without frustration! My favourite shoes are salomon.

All skilled people of all races have KUNG FU

YES YES YES YES YES YES YES YES YES YESYES YES YES YES YES YES YES YES YES YES DUI DUI DUI DUI DUI DUI DUI DUI DUI DUI DUI DUI DUI DUI DUI DUI DUI DUI YES YES YES YES YES YES YES YES YESN YES YES YES YES YES YES YES YES YES KE YI KE YI KE YI KE YI KE YI KE FI KE YI KE YI KE YI KE YI KE YI KE YI KE YI KE YI YI HOH YI HOH YI HOH YI HOH YI HOH YI HOH YI HOH YI HOH YI HOY YI HOH YI HOH YI YES YES YES YES YES YES YES YES YES YES YES YES Yes

here's a thought for aspiring sci-fi writers / aliens whisk away humans returning them as strokers. The percentage is so high the aliens glide in to claim earth with no resistance / just a bunch of disableds dishing around:)

To top this off, I must say that I am only a little **Stroker.** I am not a Physicist, Scientist, Doctor or even a Buckminster Fuller, but perhaps by having a stroke I have been exposed to Alien remembrance.

Le poem I sent to my Mum from Katoomba...

"We hopped to the rustling of the flowers And tip toed to the Lotus pond Only to find a sitting Buddha..."

Ray'yal. Ray'yaiu ¡ no L! De Raiyaws are in both Tai Chi and Music. *Everyfing de Aliens dey know si aaaaaaaaaaaaaaaaaaaaaaa.*

As an Alien, I believe there is no outside or inside.

"Sound is the Core of all Existence".

CONSULT YOUR HEALTH PROFESSIONAL AS NEEDED.

ARE WE THERE YET?

~ **THE END** ~

are you with me

~ **References and Acknowledgement** ~

Adelaide - Australia's Undiscovered Gem (Sth. Australia Tourism) A Love Supreme - John Coltrane (Impulse! Records AS-77) Autobiography of a Yogi by Paramahansa Yogananda

Barbarian Days: A Surfing Life by William Finnegan

Boy in the Bush: D.H. Lawrence - Cambridge University Press

Artist of Life - Bruce Lee edited by John Little Bruce Lee, A Life by Mathew Polly

Bruce Lee and Me (A Martial Arts Journey) - Brian Preston/Angus & Robertson

Bruce Lee - Fighting Words by Bruce Thomas/Frog Ltd.

Bruce Lee - Jeet Kune Do (DVD) Bruce Lee -

"Kung Fu, Art, Life" - HK Heritage Museum Exhibition

Bruce Lee - Words From a Master - edited by John R. Little/Contemporary Books Chans Blog - Capoeira Adelaide

Cheng Tzu's Thirteeen Treatises on T'ai Chi Ch'uan - Cheng Man Ch'ing/Blue Snake Books

Chen Taiji - Jan Silberstorff/Singing Dragon

Complete Book of Shaolin - Wong Kiew Kit/Tuttle Publishing Complete Book of Tai Chi Chuan - Wong Kiew Kit Gitanjali 35

Poem - Rabindranath Tagore

Jazz of Physics - Stephon Alexander

Journey to the Heart of Aikido by Linda Holiday/Blue Snake Books

Jungle Book (quotes from movie), Walt Disney Productions 1967

Kriya Yoga - Paramahansa Yogananda Nei Jia Quan -

Internal Martial Arts- edited by Jess O'Brien

Never Grow Up - Jackie Chan

Raga Mala - The Autobiography of Ravi Shankar

Shaolin Kung Fu

Standing Up! My Story of Hope, Advocacy and Survival After Stroke - Kathleen Jordan

Stronger after Stroke - Peter G. Levine Tai Chi (English) -

China Foreign Language bookstore. Tai Chi (Thorsons First Directions) by Paul Brecher

Tai Chi - Erle Montaigue/Carlton

Ten Methods of the Heavenly Dragon by Robert Scheaffer

The Lotus Sutra - translated by Burton Watson SGI

The Mysterious Power of Xing Yi Quan - Master CS Tang/ Singing Dragon Publishers

The Twelfth Raven - Doris Brett UWA Publishing

The Secrets of Bama - used by permission of Ma Li Yin. William Pang -

Zhao Bao Tai Chi - Unveiling the Secret of Fa Jin. William Pang -

Tai Chi Jin Mechanics - Zhao Bao Style. Cosmos Books HK

Warrior Guards the Mountain - Alex Kozma/Singing Dragon White Sands:

Experiences from the Outside World by Geoff Dyer

Yoga for People Who Can't Be Bothered to Do It by Geoff Dyer

Zero Guitar: The Science of Becoming Musical at Any Age - Gary Markus/Penguin Press

Zhaobao Taiji Quan - Master Kwan Wing Kwong

My Kung Fu

STROKE

A Memoir of Sorts by

Guy Le Claire with Chris Frazier

Chris Frazier

Chris is a 6th generation Australian born 1961 in the beautiful New England city of Armidale NSW. As a child with an inquisitive, creative and ob- serving nature, he was afforded a big area of bushland to explore and discover in. Moving to the big smoke of Sydney at the age of 10 meant quite a few changes to his life, one being exposure to some new friends, one of which was Guy Le Claire and the other was to music. His father Jim Frazier, is a self taught yet highly respected wildlife cinematographer and inventor of the Frazier Lens, well known for filming documentaries for David Attenborough has won many Australian and international awards for his work, including an Academy Award for Technical Achievement and an Emmy Award. Chris's mum Helen, grounded her family in common- sense and decency. It was with her encouragement while his father was away on filming expeditions that Chris became the *man about the house* and learned to fix all sorts of issues. Chris went on to carve an illustrious career as a professional freelance musician/bassist. With his family traits/ roots intact, those that knew him well became aware of his talent outside of performing music on technical issues, he is able to fix almost anything! No tech college for this boy! He was/is walking tech! His mind is able to confront a problem and through Frazier logic, solve it! Chris has per- formed as a musician all over Australia, Japan, Hong Kong and continues to do so. This is his first book collaboration and was made possible with the free time afforded by COVID-19 lockdowns. While it has been a learning curve, it was a pleasure to help out his old mate and brother from an- other mother Guy realise his vision and get it over the line.

Guy Le Claire

Guy Le Claire has been practising Tai Chi Chinese Kung Fu for 45 years. A notable Australian / Hong Kong musician performing for over 40 years. His Kung Fu teachers include Wing Tsun Master Po Kin Wah (Hong Kong), Grandmaster Gao (Guangxi, China) of which Guy is 4th disciple, Master Zhang Guang Wen (Shenzhen, China) who after encouraging Guy to go on and win a gold medal in 2006 and Master Pang Hon Keung (King Tai Chi Hong Kong) awarding Guy instructor status and gold in marble power 2015. As well as other HK based masters with Yim Sifu of Huo li Tai Chi Gong. Guy survived an Ischaemic stroke while based in Hong Kong in 2014, managing another year and a half in Hong Kong, he braves the occupy central demonstrations and pursues Tai Chi and Qi Gong as his pathway to recovery. In 2017 back in the Blue Mountains of Australia, he offers free classes in Tai Chi and Music, as community service. Turning 60, he completed his first book "My Kung Fu - Stroke" with schoolmate Chris Frazier and finally uploads his entire musical catalogue to **guyleclaire.bandcamp.com**. He has performed all over Asia and Australia, taking in North America and the Pacific also. Today he fiddles with Music (the sound of the Creator) and continues writing

FUCK PROCRASTINATION: "Inspiration is a guest that does not visit the lazy" – Pyotr Tsaikovsky (co/R.Malmsten).

JUST DO IT! Believe in yourself! It takes a lot of guts to get out there, play and release your product.

YESS YES YES YES YES YES YES YES YES YES YES YES YES YES YES YES YES YES YES YES YES YES YES YES YES YES I CAN YES I CAN YES I CAN CAN YES I CAN YES I CAN YES I CAN YES IS I CAN YES I CAN YES I CAN YES I CAN YES ICAN'

HAI (YES IN CANTONESE) HAI HAI HAI HAI HAI HAI HAI HAI HAI HAI HAI HAI HAI HAI HAI HAI HAI HAI HAI HAI HO YI (CAN) HO YI HO YI HO YI HO YI HO YI HO YI HO YI HO YI HO YI HO YI HO YI HO YI HO YI HO YI HO YI

DUI (YES IN MANDARIN) DUI DUI DUI DUI DUI DUI DUI DUI DUI DUI DUI DUI DUI DUI DUI DUI DUI DUI DUI DUI KE YI (CAN IN MANDO) KEYI EYI KE

YI KEYI KEYI KEYI KEYI KEYI KEYI KEYI KEYI KEYI KEYI KEYI KEYI KEYI, YES I CAN I CAN I CAN I CAN!!!!!!!!

Believe in Love, spread Love & Joy. Pure Joy/Lift!

PEACE.

See youz in the next one.

ABOUT THE AUTHOR

Retired Professional Australian /Hong Kong guitar man and Chinese kung fu enthusiast, Guy Le Claire shares his thoughts and experiences, along with history in this riveting read. Guy wrote his first book, *My Kung Fu-Stroke A Memoir of Sorts*, in Hong Kong, ultimately collaborating with Chris Frazier and finishing the book in Australia. You can discover his entire Music Catalogue at

guyleclaire.bandcamp.com and his books on Amazon.

CREDITS

I'd like to thank Leigh Johnston, Kym & Losa, Olaf and Samantha Vogee, Bellisa Evans, My Mum - Carolle Boyce, Dad - Guy senior, MaLi Yin, My Kung Fu Sifus, Kez, Simone Barry, Colin and Jill Day, Jo Truman, Dr. Jenny Brown, NDIS Anna Tardent, Dr. Philip Penfold, My Doctors yes youz, Steve Merta, Paul Chow, John Computer man, Rickard Malmsten, John Prior, Lindsay Jehan, brothers Chris Frazier, Robbin Harris and Flynn Adams, Australian Buddhist Vihara, Ulf Olafson, Dave O'Brien, and Big John Hogan and all the Musicians! Michael Smith helped edit and arrange the book. The people of Australia and Hong Kong – ga la wor! Thank You/ Dor Jay/ Ng Goi/ Xie Xie!

Brothers John Hogan, Chris Frazier, Flynn Adams and Robbin Harris – taa I love youz – u Don noodle la.

At the going down of the sun, we shall remember them.

guyleclairemusic@outlook.com

I ACKNOWLEDGE THE TRIBES AND TRIBAL ELDERS OF THIS LAND.

ARE WE THERE YET? WHERE ARE WE???

I have realised what is to be realised, I have developed what is to be developed, I have eliminated what is to be eliminated, therefore Brahmana I am the Buddha. Shakyamuni Buddha. Wasn't me! The Buddha said it.

Namo tassa bhagavato

Namo tassa bhagavato

Namo Tassa Bhagavato

Budhan saranan gachami

Dhamman saranan gachami

Sanghan saranan gachami

www.ingramcontent.com/pod-product-compliance
Lightning Source LLC
Chambersburg PA
CBHW050313010526
44107CB00055B/2221